Psychology: An Introduction

Mary E. Henry

BORU
PRESS

Boru Press Ltd
The Farmyard
Birdhill
Co. Tipperary

www.borupress.ie

© Mary E. Henry 2022

ISBN 978-1-8384134-9-1

Edited by Caitriona Clarke
Design by Sarah McCoy
Print origination by Carole Lynch
Illustrations by Andriy Yankovskyi
Printed by GraphyCems Ltd, Spain

The paper used in this book is made from wood pulp of managed forests. For every tree felled, at least one tree is planted, thereby renewing natural resources.

All rights reserved. No part of this publication may be copied, reproduced or transmitted in any form or by any means without written permission of the publishers or else under the terms of any licence permitting limited copying issued by the Irish Copyright Licensing Agency.

A CIP catalogue record for this book is available from the British Library.

For permission to reproduce photographs and artworks, the author and publisher gratefully acknowledge the following:

Alamy: 2, 6, 7, 23, 24, 29, 36, 40, 43, 44, 45, 49, 52, 58, 68, 84. iStock: 73, 78. Shutterstock: 2, 4, 10, 20, 71, 80, 83, 99, 100, 101, 102, 103.

The author and publisher have made every effort to trace all copyright holders, but if any has been inadvertently overlooked we would be pleased to make the necessary arrangement at the first opportunity.

Acknowledgements

My sincere thanks to Marion O'Brien for her support and patience throughout the process of publishing this book. Thank you to the production team at Boru Press, to Caitriona Clarke for her editorial work and to Carole Lynch for her layout work.

Finally, thank you to all the students who have inspired me over the last decade to write this book.

– Mary E. Herry

For my partner, Stephen. Thank you for your support and encouragement throughout this process.

Mary

CONTENTS

Introduction	ix
1 An Overview of Psychology	**1**
The History of Psychology	1
The Origins of Psychology	4
Psychology Becomes Scientific	6
2 The Psychoanalytic Perspective	**9**
Sigmund Freud	9
Theory of Consciousness (1915)	11
Personality Theory (1923)	12
Defence Mechanisms (1894, 1896)	13
Stages of Psychosexual Development (1905)	15
Dream Analysis (1900)	19
3 Neo-Freudianism	**22**
What is Neo-Freudianism?	22
Anna Freud	22
Carl Jung	23
Erik Erikson	29
John Bowlby	34
Therapeutic Interventions in Psychoanalysis	36
Criticisms of Psychoanalysis	38

4 The Behaviourist Perspective — 39
What is Behaviourism? — 39
Classical Conditioning — 40
John B. Watson and the 'Little Albert' Experiment — 42
B.F. Skinner and Operant Conditioning — 44
Therapeutic Interventions in Behaviourism — 46
Criticisms of Behaviourism — 47

5 Humanistic Psychology — 48
Humanism – the 'Third Force' — 48
Maslow's Hierarchy of Needs — 49
Carl Rogers and Client-Centred Therapy — 51
Therapeutic Interventions in Humanistic Psychology — 54
Criticisms of Humanistic Psychology — 56

6 The Cognitive Perspective — 57
What is Cognitive Psychology? — 57
Jean Piaget and Theory of Cognitive Development — 58
Cognitive Behavioural Therapy — 62
Albert Ellis and REBT — 62
Aaron Beck and Cognitive Therapy — 63
Lev Vygotsky and Sociocultural Theory — 67
Therapeutic Interventions in Cognitive Psychology — 68
Criticisms of Cognitive Psychology — 69

7 The Biological Perspective — 70
What is Biological Psychology? — 70
The Human Nervous System — 70

CONTENTS

The Endocrine System	80
Biological Evolution	82
Genetic Psychology	83
Therapeutic Interventions in Biological Psychology	87
Criticisms of Biological Psychology	87

8 Branches of Psychology – Developmental Psychology — 91

What is Developmental Psychology?	91
Mary Ainsworth and Attachment Styles	92
Diana Baumrind and Parenting Styles	94
Urie Bronfenbrenner and Ecological Systems	97
Lifespan Development	99
Therapeutic Interventions in Developmental Psychology	103
Criticisms of Developmental Psychology	104

9 Branches of Psychology – Abnormal Psychology — 105

What is Abnormal Psychology?	105
Determining Abnormal Behaviour	106
Diagnosing Abnormal Behaviour	109
Abnormal Disorders	110
Therapeutic Interventions in Abnormal Psychology	111
Criticisms of Abnormal Psychology	112

10 Research Methods in Psychology — 113

Scientific Method in Psychology	113
Types of Research Design in Psychology	115
Checking Validity and Reliability of Sources	119

11 Ethical Issues in Psychology and Research — 121
    Ethics in Psychology — 121
    Ethical Considerations in Research — 123

12 Working in Psychology — 127
    Interpersonal Skills — 127
    Healthy Boundaries — 129
    Self-Care — 130
    Reflection — 131

13 Case Studies — 135

14 Exam Questions with Answers — 145

Glossary of Terms — 165
Bibliography — 171
Useful Resources — 178
Index — 181

INTRODUCTION

Psychology, in the simplest of terms, is the study of the human mind and human behaviour. It is considered to be a new type of science; however, many advances have been made in the area in the last 100 years. Over this time different theorists have grappled with the subject of psychology in an attempt to explain why humans act and behave in certain ways. As human behaviour is influenced by many different factors (biological, environmental, social, cultural), there have been many debates, discussions, experiments and theories seeking to understand what drives the thoughts and actions of human beings.

Such research into the workings of the human mind and behaviour is ongoing today. Indeed, psychology is a field that is always changing and growing as the human population and world around us evolve and change.

This book looks at the origins and history of psychology. It provides a guide to the basic principles and schools of psychology and explores specific schools of thought that govern many areas of our lives today, including the areas of education, marketing, social media, communications and much more. It also applies different psychological theories and strategies to case studies to demonstrate their use and application. Whether embarking on a psychology course or simply learning and developing for personal interest, this book will help you to:

- familiarise yourself with some of the major psychology thinkers and their theories
- understand the principles of some of the major psychology perspectives and branches

PSYCHOLOGY: AN INTRODUCTION

- identify some therapeutic interventions of these psychology perspectives and branches
- consider the limitations and criticisms of these psychology perspectives
- understand the scientific process and the different types of research in the field of psychology
- explore the issues regarding ethics in psychology and research
- reflect on the interpersonal skills and knowledge needed to work in the field of psychology
- apply theoretical learning to practical situations via case studies.

chapter 1
AN OVERVIEW OF PSYCHOLOGY

IN THIS CHAPTER YOU WILL LEARN ABOUT:

- the history of psychology
- the origins of psychology
- the early schools of thought in psychology.

The History of Psychology

As evidenced by the timeline (overleaf), much has happened in the area of psychology in a relatively short period. This timeline features only some of the most important developments in the field of psychology; there are many more.

Today, there are seven well-known perspectives in psychology:

1. The Psychoanalytic (or Psychodynamic) Perspective
2. The Behavioural Perspective
3. The Cognitive Perspective
4. The Biological Perspective
5. The Cross-Cultural Perspective
6. The Evolutionary Perspective
7. The Humanistic Perspective.

2 PSYCHOLOGY: AN INTRODUCTION
TIMELINE OF PSYCHOLOGY

1879: Wilhelm Wundt opens the first psychology lab in Germany

1898: The School of Structuralism is developed by Edward Titchener arising from work of Wundt

1899: The School of Functionalism is founded by William James in reaction to Structuralism

1900: Dream interpretation and psychoanalysis is introduced in Sigmund Freud's book *The Interpretation of Dreams*

1913: John B. Watson starts Behaviourism

1935: Gestalt psychology is launched by Kurt Koffka

1938: B.F. Skinner introduces operant psychology as part of Behaviourism

1946: Anna Freud introduces the treatment of children with child psychoanalysis

1951: The first drug to treat depression is approved by the US Food and Drug Administration (FDA)

1952: The first Diagnostic and Statistical Manual (DSM) for mental disorders is published in the USA

1953: The first ethical standards in psychology are published by the American Psychological Association, entitled *Ethical Principles of Psychologists and Code of Conduct*

1954: Humanistic psychology is established by Carl Rogers and Abraham Maslow

1956: Cognitive psychology is established by Ulric Neisser, influenced by the work of George A. Miller, Aaron Beck, Jean Piaget and others

1957: Jane Goodall begins her studies of primates

1960/1963: The FDA approves the drugs Librium and Valium for anxiety and other mood disorders

1968: DSM-II is published

1976: Evolutionary psychology takes root as Richard Dawkins publishes work on genes and evolution

1980: DSM-III is published

1990: Cultural psychology is founded by Jerome Bruner

1990: Human genome mapping begins

1994: DSM-IV is published

1998: Positive psychology is founded by Martin Seligman

2013: DSM-V is published

AN OVERVIEW OF PSYCHOLOGY

Each perspective has its own theories and areas of focus and different branches of psychology have developed from them. However, they all have the common goal of trying to understand human thoughts, feelings and behaviours in order to help a person overcome difficulties. The psychoanalytic, behaviourist, cognitive, biological and humanistic perspectives will be explored in more detail in this book.

Psychology is an ever-changing and evolving entity. It is a field that encompasses the areas of research and practice. Various psychological perspectives conduct research in order to gain more understanding of human behaviour with the hope of applying this learning and understanding to real-life situations with clients.

Task

Think-Pair-Share

Can you think of some areas where psychology is used today? Perhaps you are interested in one of these areas yourself. Think about it for a few moments, fill in the mind map, then pair with a classmate and share what you came up with.

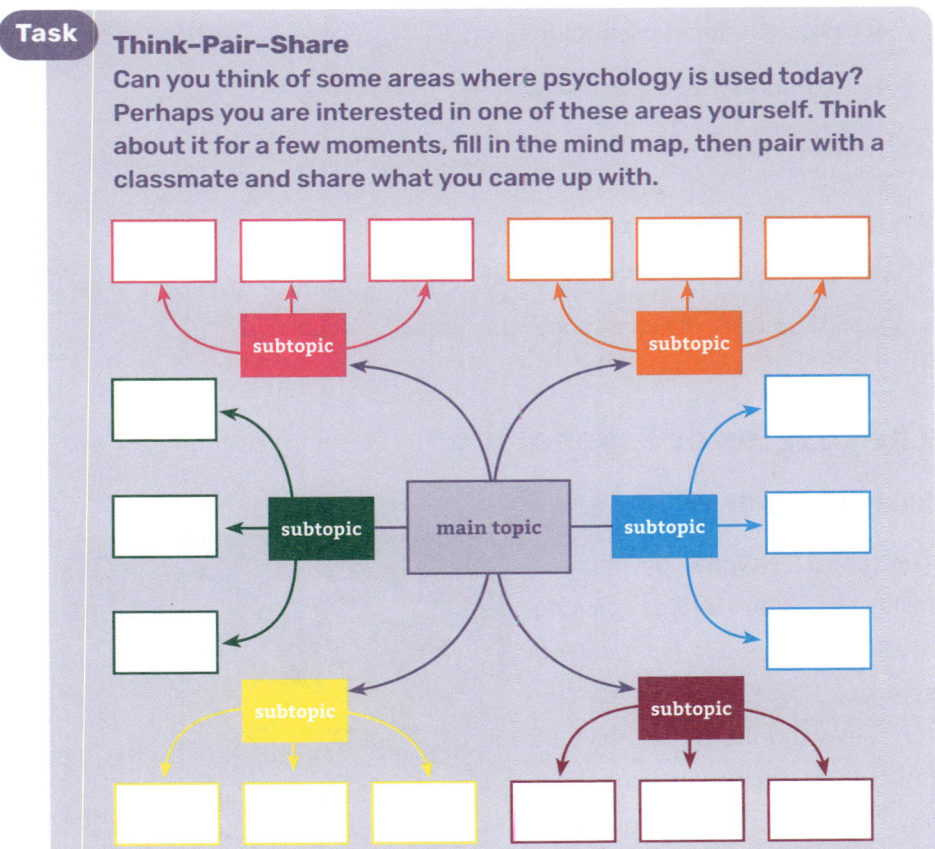

Psychology branches include:

+ developmental psychology
+ educational psychology
+ sports psychology
+ biopsychology
+ clinical psychology
+ comparative psychology
+ counselling psychology
+ health psychology
+ forensic psychology
+ organisational psychology
+ experimental psychology.

REFLECT

What area or field of psychology are you interested in?

Why are you interested in that area?

What do you already know about that area of psychology?

The Origins of Psychology

Early Psychology

The word 'psychology' comes from the Greek words *psyche* meaning soul and *logos* meaning science. Psychology in its raw form evolved from the field of philosophy. Philosophy, meaning 'love of wisdom', is the study of

questioning the nature of humankind. Great philosophers like Socrates, Plato and Aristotle spent many hours discussing human motivation, and from this time period of 300–500 BCE up to the present day, great thinkers have attempted to explain and understand concepts such as nature versus nurture and destiny versus free will. For example, in relation to the nature–nurture debate, Plato argued in defence of the nature principle, believing that thoughts and behaviours were driven by innate instincts or genetics. Conversely, Aristotle believed that nurture or the environment was mostly responsible for our thoughts and behaviours.

> **Task** **Think-Pair-Share**
> What are your views on the nature–nurture debate? Are our thoughts and behaviours influenced more by our DNA or by our environment? Pair and share your thoughts.

The nature–nurture debate was the main focus of early psychology until about the sixteenth century. During the seventeenth century, philosophers such as René Descartes and John Locke advanced the nature–nurture theory, bringing into existence and debating new concepts such as dualism. Developed by Descartes, dualism proposed that the body and mind were two separate entities. Locke, however, disagreed with this concept of separation, arguing that physical processes such as thoughts and feelings happened in the brain and were experienced by the body; therefore, no separation took place.

The debate surrounding the roles of nature or nurture in human development is ongoing today, with many theorists falling into either one or the other camp. The big question for many psychologists has always been: Are we born with the traits and characteristics that shape us as individuals, or do we develop these traits and characteristics because of our environment?

Psychology Becomes Scientific

Even though it could be argued that the first psychological experiments took place in 700 BCE, the modern scientific process of looking at the human mind formally began in 1879 when Wilhelm Wundt established the first psychology laboratory in Leipzig, Germany. Often called the father of psychology, Wundt had a huge influence on the development of the field, particularly in the USA. His life's work was vast and included writings on philosophy and physiology as well as on psychology.

Two of the earliest schools of psychology were structuralism and functionalism. Neither of these schools exist today but they have influenced other areas of psychology.

Structuralism – Wundt and Titchener

Structuralism was the first major school of thought in psychology. In essence, it grounded psychology as a separate discipline to philosophy. Established by Wundt and developed by his student Edward Titchener, structuralism focused on the idea of introspection and the breakdown of the mental processes of the mind.

Focus on … Wilhelm Wundt (1832–1920)

Wilhelm Wundt was born in Mannheim, Germany, in 1832. The son of a Lutheran pastor, Wilhelm attended the University of Heidelberg, where he received a degree in medicine. As time went on, his interests turned towards sensory processes and perception. This led to an interest in psychology, and he founded what is regarded as the first laboratory of experimental psychology at the

University of Leipzig in 1879. Wundt was a writer as well as a researcher, publishing almost 500 articles and books in his lifetime.

Functionalism – William James

Functionalism was developed by the American psychologist William James in reaction to structuralism. Influenced by the works of Charles Darwin and John Dewey, this school of psychology focused on understanding the biological processes behind and purpose of human consciousness. It would go on to be very influential on the educational system and the concept that children learn in developmental stages.

Focus on ... William James (1842–1910)

William James was one of the most influential of the early American psychologists. After completing his medical degree at Harvard University, he began his teaching career in physiology at Harvard, but over time added more psychological content, so that by 1878 the course was completely psychology-focused. At that time he began writing a psychology textbook. Taking over ten years to complete, *The Principles of Psychology* (1890) is considered the first  book on the topic of psychology. It would go on to become one of the best-known and most-read texts in the field of psychology and is still in print today.

PSYCHOLOGY: AN INTRODUCTION

Review what you have learned

1. Who were the first psychologists?
2. Why was psychology developed?
3. Who is known as the father of psychology?
4. Where was the first psychology lab built?
5. Name two early schools of psychology and their founders.

chapter 2
THE PSYCHOANALYTIC PERSPECTIVE

IN THIS CHAPTER YOU WILL LEARN ABOUT:

- Sigmund Freud and the principles of psychoanalysis
- the theory of consciousness
- the parts of the personality according to psychoanalysis
- defence mechanisms
- the psychosexual stages
- dream analysis.

Sigmund Freud

Known as the father of psychoanalysis, Sigmund Freud began his career treating people with brain damage. At the time, brain damage was treated under the area of hysteria – defined as the exhibition of physical symptoms with no apparent physical cause.

Using many techniques to treat hysteria – with mixed results – Freud (1895) noted the work of other doctors who used hypnosis in treatment and eventually began to have breakthroughs using the technique himself. He discovered that if a patient remembered a traumatic event, it led to an emotional release known as catharsis. He eventually discarded the use of hypnosis altogether and began asking patients to say whatever came to mind – a technique now widely known as free association. These words or thoughts would then, Freud believed, unlock memories that had been repressed or blocked by the patient. Unlocking these repressed memories would initially cause physical symptoms for the person, which would resolve themselves as the memory was processed. Freud believed that behaviour always had a cause, even if it wasn't understood. This was the beginning of the field of psychoanalysis.

Focus on ... Sigmund Freud (1856–1939)

Sigmund Freud was born in 1856 in the Moravian town of Freiberg in what was then the Austrian Empire. The eldest of eight children, Freud studied physiology at the University of Vienna. He was interested in research, but the responsibilities of family life and the need for greater financial security led him to become a doctor. In 1885 Freud received a fellowship to study with Jean Charcot, a French neurologist best known for his work on hypnosis and hysteria. Working with Charcot, Freud learned about hysteria disorders and techniques of hypnosis.

On returning to Vienna to practise, he specialised in neurological disorders (including hysteria), and became a leading figure in the area – a focus which eventually led to his search for new treatments and explanations. In 1919, he was granted the title of Professor at the University of Vienna. He died in 1939, at the age of 83, in London.

Theory of Consciousness (1915)

Freud's View of the Human Mind: The Mental Iceberg

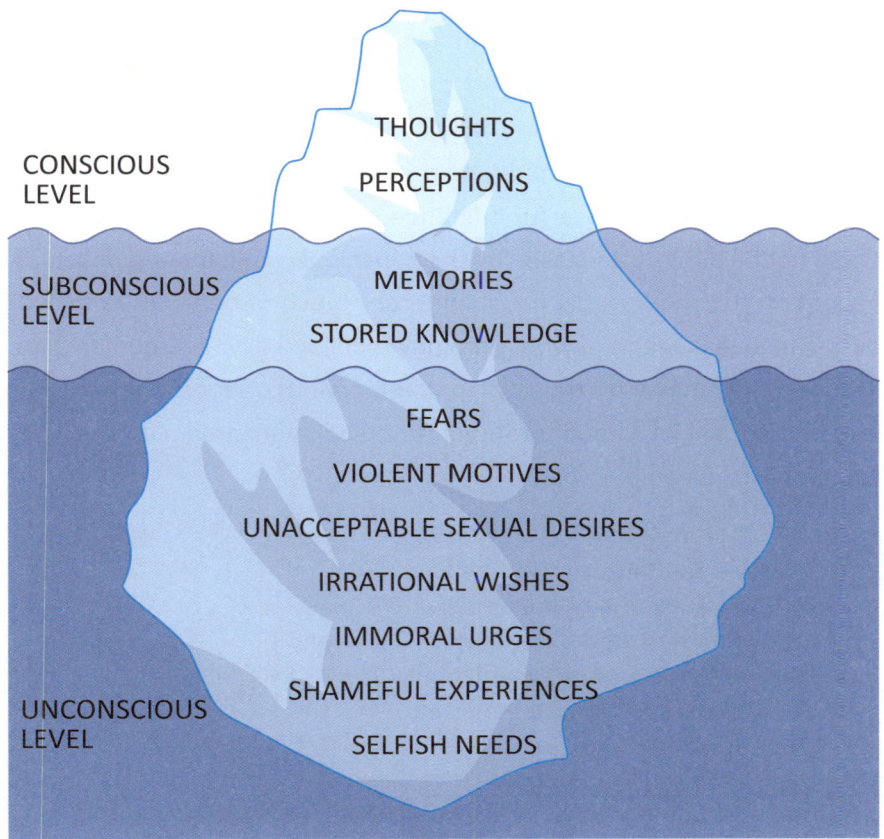

Emerging theories and thoughts regarding the link between repressed memories and behaviour led Freud to examine consciousness and the mind. He believed that awareness was divided into different parts of consciousness. The things that we are aware of at any given moment occur at the level of the conscious mind (above the surface). Freud believed that about ten per cent of our thoughts and experiences existed here.

Those thoughts that remained hidden or obscured existed in the subconscious mind (below the surface), which Freud theorised was made up of two parts: the preconscious mind and the unconscious mind.

The preconscious mind consists of thoughts, events and experiences that can be recalled and brought back into awareness quite easily, for example, feelings about starting a new course of study or job. The unconscious mind consists of those thoughts and experiences that are more deeply buried, pushed down and repressed. For Freud, the unconscious was a powerful influence on behaviour: even though it could not be directly accessed by the conscious mind, the unconscious, according to Freud, would cause different types of behaviours to 'leak out'. These leakages are what are known colloquially as Freudian slips. Freud spent much of his time with patients trying to access the contents of their unconscious mind through free association, dream analysis and transference (see next chapter).

> **Task** **Think-Pair-Share**
> Can you think of any examples of Freudian slips? Pair and share any examples you might be aware of from everyday life, TV, movies, etc.

Personality Theory (1923)

Freud's work on the mind led to the analysis of personality. He divided the concept of personality into three parts: the id, the ego and the superego.

Id	Ego	Superego
The part of personality concerned with basic needs and drives. The id relates to primal nature, thinking only about gratification. (Think of the devil on your shoulder.) It is ruled by the gratification principle, which states that instant gratification is all that matters.	The part of the personality that mediates between the id and the superego. It is concerned with the reality principle: it must assess the reality of the external world and act accordingly, while trying to balance the demands of the id and the superego.	The part of the personality concerned with the conscience, driven by morals and what is considered right and wrong. (Think of the angel on your shoulder.) The superego aims for perfection and its demands often oppose those of the id's.

Freud believed that the continual balancing act between the id and the superego is what determines different behaviours to emerge within the personality. These behaviours will be unique to each individual. When anxiety arises in the ego because of the pushing demands of the id, defence mechanisms will be put in place by the person.

Defence Mechanisms (1894, 1896)

Another of Freud's contributions to psychology is the well-known concept of defence mechanisms. As the ego tries to mediate between the desires of the id and the moral conscience of the superego, difficulties can arise in the personality in the form of conflict. Freud said that these conflicts create anxiety in the person. In an attempt to avoid or protect oneself from anxiety, the person develops coping skills that are often unconscious to them.

Here are some well-known defence mechanisms and examples.

- **Denial:** Refusing to see the facts in a situation.
For example: You smoke every day and have now developed breathing problems. Your doctor has advised you to stop smoking

as it is exacerbating the condition. However, you do not believe that smoking is the cause of your breathing difficulties.

- **Displacement:** Expressing inappropriate urges or behaviour on a less-threatening target.
  For example: Your boss tells you that you have yet again failed to meet your monthly targets and that you will face disciplinary action if things do not improve. You are angry with your boss but say nothing. When you arrive home your dog jumps up to greet you and in response you kick him.

- **Regression:** Going back to coping mechanisms that you used in childhood.
  For example: You receive news that you did not get a job offer you really wanted. To comfort yourself, you revert to your childhood habit of thumb sucking.

- **Sublimation:** Focusing unacceptable feelings or emotions into acceptable activities or causes.
  For example: When feeling the need to fight or be aggressive with someone, a person goes to the gym or a boxing class instead.

- **Reaction formation:** Replacing an unwanted impulse or anxiety with the opposite reaction.
  For example: The young boy who is attracted to a girl pulls her hair instead of being kind to her.

- **Projection:** Giving our own unacceptable feelings or qualities to another person.
  For example: Disliking a person but believing they dislike you.

- **Repression:** Blocking out painful experiences from the past.
  For example: Having a fear of dogs as an adult because of a frightening experience with them as a child but having no recollection of this experience.

THE PSYCHOANALYTIC PERSPECTIVE

+ **Rationalisation:** Logically trying to explain something that is painful or unacceptable.
  For example: When a promotion has not been offered, saying that the extra responsibility was not wanted in any case.

Freud believed that everyone used defence mechanisms and that their use was to a certain extent healthy and necessary. However, an excessive use of defence mechanisms indicated an inability on the part of the person to deal maturely with life's issues and led to a worsening of such problems.

Task: Think-Pair-Share
Come up with other examples of these defence mechanisms, then pair and share your examples.

Defence Mechanism	Example
Denial	
Displacement	
Regression	
Sublimation	
Reaction formation	
Projection	
Repression	
Rationalisation	

Stages of Psychosexual Development (1905)

Freud believed that as a person grew from child to adult, conflicts within the id, ego and superego changed and progressed through a series of five basic stages: oral, anal, phallic, latency and genital. This is known as the psychosexual theory of development. Three terms used by Freud within this theory were:

- **Libido:** Sexual energy that is created through different types of behaviours
- **Erogenous zone:** A part of the body that is sensitive to touch
- **Fixation:** The idea that part of a person's libido is stuck in a particular stage of development because of overindulgence or a blockage.

Each of the five psychosexual stages was believed to be directly related to a different physical centre of pleasure or erogenous zone. Across these five stages, the person is presented with different conflicts between their biological drives (id) and their moral conscience (superego) because their biological pleasure-seeking urges – their libido – grow and change over time. The person will look for satisfaction through different types of behaviours using these erogenous zones; for example, in the oral stage the baby will suck their thumb for oral stimulation.

The person's ability to resolve the conflicts present in each stage indicates how successful they will be in the functional world. Freud believed that failure to resolve a conflict within a stage could cause a person to have a fixation in that stage, leading to unhealthy personality traits. For example, the person in the oral stage who does not resolve the conflict of oral stimulation (weaning) will have an oral fixation in later life, which might manifest in nail-biting, smoking, finger-chewing, etc. Conversely, Freud believed, successful resolution of the stages would lead to a healthy, integrated personality and individual.

1. Oral Stage

The oral stage occurs from birth until about 18 months. The erogenous zone for this stage is the mouth. At this stage, young babies and toddlers are known for putting everything in their mouths, from their rattle to their fingers, and so on. This age group finds pleasure in sucking and chewing, and these desires are driven by the id, which is constantly seeking to be satisfied. Babies in this stage are nurtured and fed through breastfeeding or bottle feeding. They have a large dependence on their carer for food and enjoy the feeding experience. As they grow in this stage, they will usually be weaned off of breast or bottle feeding and will be eased into eating solid foods. If they do not go through the weaning process correctly, according to this theory, they will later develop oral fixations.

2. Anal Stage

The anal stage happens at around 18 months and continues until age three. The erogenous zone is the anus. At this stage, toddlers potty train and learn how to control their bowel movements. The ego starts to form, managing the demands of the id. According to the theory, if the parent is too demanding and controlling of the child in potty training, the child may come to have an anal fixation later in life. This anal fixation is often termed 'anal compulsive' and Freud believed that it manifested in a strong need to organise, clean and keep everything in order. On the other hand, if the parent is deemed too lax with the child in their approach to potty training, the child will have an 'anal expulsive' pattern of behaviour where they will lack organisation and tidiness.

3. Phallic Stage

The phallic stage happens between the ages of three and six. The erogenous zone is the genitals. A child starts to discover these parts of their body and explores these areas with curiosity. Freud believed that the superego developed at this stage, enabling a child to understand the difference between right and wrong in a moral way. In this stage, Freud believed that boys went through the Oedipus complex. This is a process in which a boy is jealous of his father and desires to be with his mother in a sexual way. Freud believed that the boy eventually has to make peace with these strong feelings and identify with the father in order to proceed smoothly to the stage. Girls, Freud maintained, similarly desired their father and were jealous of their mother. This is known as the Electra complex. Freud also theorised that all women had penis envy, whereby young girls experience anxiety upon realising that they do not have a penis. (This has become very controversial over time, with many theorists and psychoanalysts disputing its validity.) If development is interrupted in this stage, Freud theorised, a person in later life may have problems with their moral code and reasoning.

4. Latency Stage

This stage lasts from age six to about 12 or 13. In this stage the child does not have any active erogenous zones – they lie dormant as the child develops. Throughout this stage the child puts their focus on schoolwork and chores and has time to explore their personality before puberty. Fixations from other stages may become noticeable in this stage and a child may start to show behaviours like thumb sucking or a compulsion for organising.

5. Genital Stage

The final stage of Freud's five-stage psychosexual theory lasts from puberty until death. The erogenous zone is the genitals and concerns sexual intercourse. In this stage a person looks for a partner with whom to create intimacy and to reproduce. The superego fully develops and allows the person to balance their desires and needs. If the person does not master this stage, according to the theory, they may have difficulties in finding or maintaining a romantic relationship.

THE PSYCHOANALYTIC PERSPECTIVE

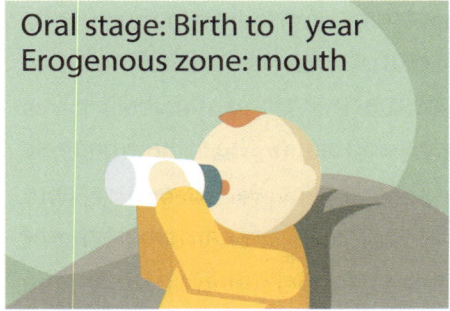

Oral stage: Birth to 1 year
Erogenous zone: mouth

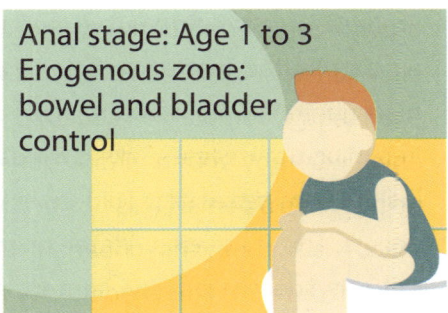

Anal stage: Age 1 to 3
Erogenous zone: bowel and bladder control

Phallic stage: Age 3 to 6
Erogenous zone: genitals

Latency stage: 6 to puberty
Libido inactive

Genital stage: Puberty to death
maturing sexual interests

Dream Analysis (1900)

Freud believed that dream interpretation was the 'royal road' to the unconscious. In other words, our dreams are a gateway to what we are storing and are not aware of in the unconscious mind. The purpose of the dream state is to fulfil the wishes of the unconscious mind. During the waking day the person may experience childlike wishes or desires from the id, which are suppressed by the ego. The dream state, however, can express these wishes or fantasies because the sleeping mind does not censor thoughts and desires.

Freud believed that these wishes played out in symbolic ways in dreams and attributed many symbols to a person's sexual life. For Freud, the male genitals were linked to any objects that were long and phallus-like, including umbrellas, sticks, swords, guns and so on. The female genitals included things that could be filled, including caves, boxes, treasure chests and suitcases. Water nearly always symbolised some type of birth, and death was represented by a pilgrimage or journey. In treatment, Freud would ask the patient to calmly recite everything they remembered about their dream using free association. He would then spend time analysing the manifest or literal content of the dream and interpreting symbols to uncover the latent or hidden content of the dream.

Dream interpretation is still used by some psychologists today, while others do not believe that the practice holds weight.

REFLECT

Can you remember any dream you had recently? Did anything stand out in the dream?

Do you have a recurring dream? Do you think your dreams are trying to tell you something?

Sigmund Freud made a lasting impact on the field of psychology as we know it today. Whether you agree or disagree with his work, its influence is felt in many areas. Most of Freud's work was tailored around the individual and he garnered much of his information from his one-to-one work with them. Major thinkers have contributed work that grew out of his legacy, while others have developed new theories in opposition to his ideas.

THE PSYCHOANALYTIC PERSPECTIVE

Review what you have learned

1. Create a chart or cartoon to describe the id, the ego and the superego as explained by Freud.
2. What, according to Freud, led to the development of an oral fixation?
3. Explain what is meant by the Oedipus and Electra complexes.
4. Summarise the rationale behind dream analysis.

chapter 3
NEO-FREUDIANISM

IN THIS CHAPTER YOU WILL LEARN ABOUT:

- Anna Freud and psychoanalysis
- Carl Jung, personality theory and dream analysis
- Erik Erikson and psychosocial development
- John Bowlby and attachment theory
- therapeutic interventions in psychoanalysis
- criticisms of psychoanalysis.

What is Neo-Freudianism?

Sigmund Freud proposed many ideas that were highly controversial, but he also attracted a great many followers. Neo-Freudian psychologists were thinkers who agreed with many of the core principles of Freud's psychoanalytic theory but adapted the approach to incorporate their own ideas, beliefs and opinions. Neo-Freudianism is therefore a psychoanalytical approach deriving from the influence of Freud but extending his theories towards social or cultural aspects of psychoanalysis over a biological approach. Some major neo-Freudian psychologists include Anna Freud, Carl Jung, Erik Erikson and John Bowlby.

Anna Freud

Anna Freud was the originator of child psychoanalysis as a distinct form of therapy. She believed that child therapy should operate according to the basic principles of psychoanalysis, with children starting therapy only when they reached the latency stage (around the age of six). Before that, she thought it best to focus on the child's environment to support their holistic development. Freud maintained the importance of creating a strong therapeutic bond with children. She was also sensitive to the fact that, unlike adults who usually seek help on their own, children can rarely operate as autonomous individuals. This first stage of focusing on and interacting with the child's environment was intended to gain children's attention and trust before starting any therapy with them.

Focus on ... Anna Freud (1895–1982)

The youngest child of Sigmund Freud and Martha Bernays, Anna Freud was born in Vienna in 1895. Starting out her career as a schoolteacher, she went on to become a psychoanalyst working with children. She also developed her father's work on defence mechanisms, publishing a book on the topic in 1936. Freud's experience of working with children during wartime has had a lasting impact on the field of child psychoanalysis generally and several of her publications have influenced the area of play therapy. The war nursery she opened in Hampstead for children of single parents later became a clinic for child therapy. Renamed the Anna Freud Centre after her death in 1982, this centre is still open today, offering mental health support to children, young people and their families.

Carl Jung

Carl Jung was a student of Sigmund Freud and was influenced by his work and theories. Jung's work focused on the areas of the psyche, personality, dream analysis and archetypes. He believed that the psyche was divided into three parts: the ego, the personal unconscious and the collective unconscious.

Ego	Personal unconscious	Collective unconscious
Everything that creates consciousness – all of the unrepressed thoughts, feelings and emotions of a person.	The repressed thoughts, feelings and emotions of a person. Jung believed that the personal unconscious was not too far from the ego mind and could be easily accessed.	The repressed thoughts, feelings and emotions of the collective. Jung, unlike Freud, believed that specific cultures held ancestral patterns and memories that were universal.

Focus on ... Carl Jung (1875–1961)

Carl Gustav Jung was born in Switzerland in 1875. The son of a pastor, his family counted a number of clergymen among its members. Breaking with tradition, Jung went into the field of medicine, studying in Basel and Zurich and becoming a psychiatrist. While working at an asylum, he took the opportunity to study some of his patients, which resulted in findings that were along similar lines to those of Sigmund Freud. This led to him working with Freud for about five years; however, the two eventually parted ways, owing to disagreements on theoretical content as well as differing personalities. Jung published over thirty books in the area of psychology and countless others in science-related fields. He is best known for his work on personality, archetypes and the collective unconscious.

Personality Theory (1933, 1947)

Archetypes, according to Jung, were universal knowledge and ideals passed down from our ancestors and held in the collective unconscious. They are unlearned and their function is to organise how we experience certain things. Jung believed that every person had four archetypes in their personality.

The Four Jungian Archetypes (1947)

1. **The persona:** According to Jung, the persona is the different masks we wear in order to fit in in society. We have various personas depending on who we are with and they change depending on the context, culture and overall environment.

2. **The shadow:** The shadow is the repressed side of ourselves, the thoughts, feelings and memories that we repress for various reasons. It resides in our unconscious and we are not aware of it. This concept was inspired by Freud's work on the unconscious mind.

3. **The anima/animus:** The anima is the ideal woman in a man's psyche and represents femininity, while the animus is the ideal man in the woman's psyche and represents masculinity. Culture and society shape our concepts of what is the 'ideal', and we project that on to the opposite gender.

4. **The self:** When the ego unites the conscious and unconscious states, an individual becomes a whole self. This is also called the process of individuation, whereby the person becomes a united, integrated person.

Jung was a pioneer in the area of personality. His concepts are now widely used in modern popular psychology. He was one of the first people to define the terms 'introvert' and 'extrovert' in the psychological context. According to him, an introvert is a person who gets their energy from an inward focus and prefers time alone. They are usually shyer and avoid the limelight. An extrovert, on the other hand, gets their energy from those around them and they project their energy outward. They are usually highly social and enjoy being the centre of attention. Jung went on to develop four different ways of interacting as an introvert or extrovert: sensing, feeling, intuiting and thinking.

This general classification is today seen as overly simplistic, but Jung's theories have been modified and are well known and used in personality tests, including the very well-known Myers–Briggs test.

> **MYERS–BRIGGS PERSONALITY TEST**
>
> Developed by Isabel Myers and her mother Katherine Briggs, this personality test is a self-reported inventory that attempts to assign four categories: introvert or extrovert; sensing or intuition; thinking or feeling; and judging or perceiving. One letter is taken from each category to produce a four-letter code assigning personality type, of which there are 16 in total:
>
> | | | |
> |---|---|---|
> | the inspector | the crafter | the protector |
> | the artist | the advocate | the mediator |
> | the architect | the thinker | the persuader |
> | the director | the performer | the caregiver |
> | the champion | the giver | the debater |
> | the commander | | |

REFLECT

Today new theories posit that someone can be an 'ambivert', which is a hybrid of an introvert and an extrovert. Do you think you are an introvert, an extrovert or an ambivert?

Have you taken the Myers–Briggs personality test or any other personality test? Do you think there is any validity in these tests?

Dream Analysis (1933)

Carl Jung once said, 'The dream is a little hidden door in the innermost and most secret recesses of the soul.' Jung disagreed with Freud about the general symbolism of dreams. Believing that Freud put too much emphasis on the sexual nature of dreams, Jung instead thought that the libido was not sexual energy but psychic energy. He felt that dreams gave the person a window into their personal and collective unconscious, a way to uncover what was truly going on in their unconscious mind. The symbolism in the dream was unique to the person. Jung worked a lot with the concept of archetypes in dream interpretation.

Jung's 12 Archetypes

Jung believed that the collective unconscious held 12 universal personality archetypes.

1. **Ruler:** Boss, leader, manager. Strives for power and control.
2. **Creator:** Artist, writer, musician, poet. Strives to create beauty and things that will endure in time.
3. **Sage:** Philosopher, mentor, teacher, researcher. Strives for wisdom and truth.
4. **Innocent:** Mystic, saint, dreamer. Strives for innocence and happiness.
5. **Explorer:** Adventure seeker, mountain climber, seeker. Strives for freedom to explore the world and discover new things.
6. **Rebel:** Wild man/woman, revolutionary. Strives to create change and revolution.
7. **Hero:** Warrior, fireman/woman, soldier. Strives to do courageous and noble acts.

PSYCHOLOGY: AN INTRODUCTION

8 **Wizard:** Shaman, healer, visionary, inventor. Strives to understand the universe.

9 **Jester:** Joker, comedian, class clown. Strives to make others laugh and to entertain.

10 **Everyman:** Worker, neighbour, underdog. Strives for connection with others.

11 **Lover:** Team builder, partner, cheerleader, friend. Strives for experience and intimate connections.

12 **Caregiver:** Parent, supporter, activist, volunteer. Strives to protect and care for others.

Task

Think-Pair-Share

The use of archetypes is very clear to see in marketing and branding, and businesses and companies frequently use psychology and its understanding of human behaviour to create, target and drive advertising campaigns in order to sell more goods and services. Can you think of any examples of archetypes being utilised in the brands you use every day? The following table features some examples. See if you can add more, then pair and share what you come up with.

Archetype	Brand 1 Example	Brand 2 Example	Brand 3 Example
Creator	Lego		
Sage	Oprah Winfrey/ Harpo Productions		
Explorer	Regatta		
Hero	Nike – 'Just do it!'		

Erik Erikson

Erik Erikson met Anna Freud after dropping out of art school and going to teach at her school for children in Vienna. It was there that he became interested in the field of psychoanalysis. Erikson is considered a neo-Freudian because he used Freud's psychoanalytic theory to develop his own theory of psychosocial stages. He believed that the personality developed through eight fixed stages of psychosocial development, from infancy to adulthood. During each stage the person goes through a psychosocial crisis that can have either a positive or negative outcome on the development of the personality.

Focus on ... Erik Erikson (1902–1994)

Erik Homburger Erikson was born in 1902 in Frankfurt, Germany. He was raised by his single mother, who became pregnant with Erik following an extramarital affair. She later married a doctor, whom Erik believed for many years to be his biological father. On finding out that he was not, Erik reported feeling lost and confused about his identity, a situation exacerbated by the separation he felt from his Jewish peers owing to his blond hair and blue eyes. He would go on to coin the term 'identity crisis'.

Erikson worked with Anna Freud and learned more about the field of psychoanalysis. Freud saw that he had a natural way with children and encouraged him to study and learn more. He lectured at Harvard and other universities and wrote a number of books. Erikson is best known for his development of the theory of the eight psychosocial stages of development.

Eight Stages of Psychosocial Development (1968)

More than Freud or Jung, Erikson shifted the focus of development more to the person's interaction with society. As an individual develops, society places new demands on them. Erikson theorised that there were eight stages of psychosocial development, with each stage involving certain developmental outcomes known as tasks, which are psycho (mind) and social (society) in nature. These stages represent a crisis or conflict between the self and the burdens society places on the self.

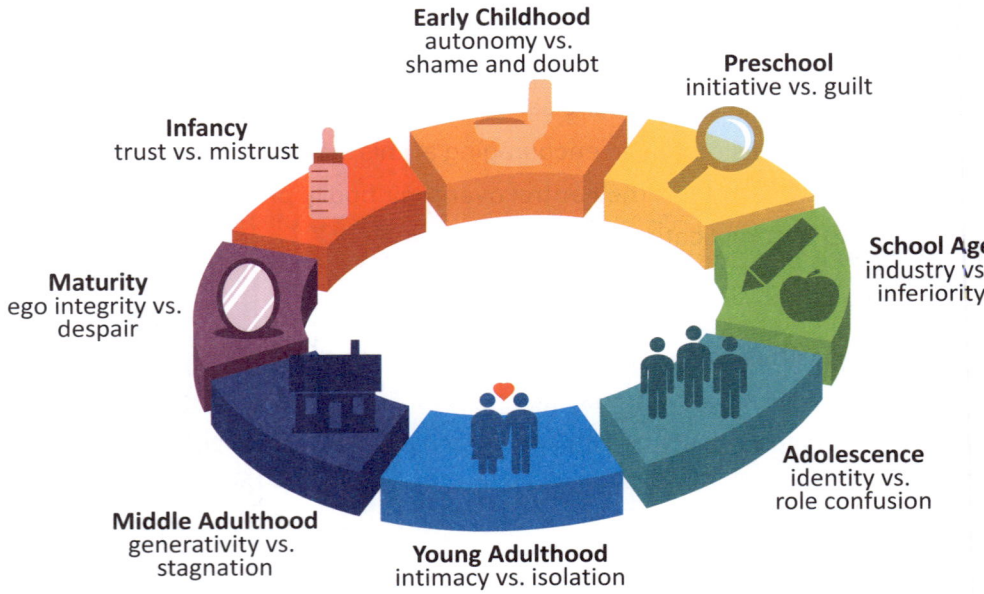

Stage 1: Trust versus Mistrust

This stage begins at birth and finishes at around 18 months. The conflict at this stage is whether to trust others or not. At this stage the caregiver needs to provide consistent care for the child to trust. If a child has trust in the caregiver they will go on to feel more secure and safe in the world and will develop the outcome of hope as the world will feel like a welcoming and supportive place. If a caregiver is inconsistent and unavailable at the early stages of development the child will not feel safe or secure, will fear the outside world and will not develop the outcome of hope.

Stage 2: Autonomy versus Shame and Doubt

This stage starts at about 18 months and continues to age three. In this stage the child is going through toilet training. Erikson believed that if a child could learn to regulate their bodily functions at this stage they would gain more autonomy in themselves. If a parent is encouraging and supportive at this stage then a child will develop the outcome of will. If a caregiver allows the child to control their motor skills and feed and dress themselves as well as choosing their own toys they will move on to the next stage with more ease and confidence. If a caregiver is not supportive, consistent and encouraging at this stage then the child will not gain these skills or the control over their bodily processes and this may lead to complications as they progress.

Stage 3: Initiative versus Guilt

This stage starts at age three and ends at about age five. These are the preschool years, and at this stage the child needs to find their own sense of responsibility and independence and be given the opportunity to take on initiative. The caregiver needs to allow the child to assert their own power and take on role playing, directing play and other social interactions. If the child is not allowed to direct some interactions or not encouraged to take on a leading role in cleaning up toys, for example, they will not achieve the outcome of a sense of purpose in the world and may end up feeling guilty about trying to assert themselves or reluctant to take on new challenges.

Stage 4: Industry versus Inferiority

This stage starts at about age five and ends at about age 12. These are the school-going years, when the child is beginning to focus on tasks outside the home and immediate family. Now a child needs to be successful in the school setting and in the multiple roles in which they find themselves. If the caregiver and teachers assist the child in having an enjoyable and productive experience at school the child will develop the outcome of competence. If the child has a negative school experience then they will not develop a sense of competence.

> **Task** **Think-Pair-Share**
> What are some reasons that a child may have a negative school experience? Consider the following: relationships with friends and teachers; the school culture; parental involvement; school facilities. Pair and share your thoughts.

Stage 5: Identity versus Role Confusion

This stage starts at about age 12 and ends at about age 18. This is the adolescent stage of development. During these teenage years the adolescent starts to move away from their parents and develop their own ideas, values and morals. The caregiver is less prominent in shaping the life of the adolescent, who begins to make other meaningful relationships and explore their own identity outside of the nuclear family. This is a time of negotiating rules and trying to fit in or not. If an adolescent does not figure out their identity at this stage they will not achieve fidelity (a sense of faithfulness to others, to causes and beliefs, etc.) or a sense of freedom and trust within themselves.

Stage 6: Intimacy versus Isolation

This stage starts at about age 19 and ends at approximately age 40. In this stage people look to settle down and start families of their own. The young adult now looks to find a mate and to share intimacy with this person and with others in their circle of friends. Many people in this stage create a home and partnership with a significant other and become parents themselves, leading to the outcome of love. If this does not happen in this stage it can lead to isolation.

Stage 7: Generativity versus Stagnation

This stage starts at age 40 and continues until age 65. In this stage the most important things are family and career. During middle adulthood the person strives to give back and make a difference that is lasting to society, meeting the outcome of care. Many people in this stage will multitask between being caregivers to their own families and finding a purpose that is important to them in the larger society. This could be in a career, vocation or volunteer work. If a person does not find that purpose they may stagnate in their development.

Stage 8: Integrity versus Despair

At this last stage the most important task for a person is reflection. Here a person reviews their life and their accomplishments. If they are happy with the outcomes of their life they will feel proud and will experience the outcome of wisdom. If they regret their choices they must find a way to make peace with them or they may suffer depression and despair.

REFLECT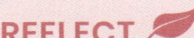

What would you like to achieve when you look back on your life at stage 8? Consider this and see whether you can start laying the groundwork now!

Apply your learning

In groups, read the following case studies and list some tips or suggestions you might give to parents/caregivers following what you have learned from Erikson's stages theory.

> **Case study 1: Aoife**
>
> Aoife is eight months and is in stage 1 of Erikson's theory. Aoife is being raised by her father and he is bottle feeding.
>
> What tips or suggestions would you give to him to support Aoife in this stage?
>
> **Case study 2: Maeve**
>
> Maeve is two years six months and is in stage 2 of Erikson's theory. She is wetting the bed most nights and is getting very upset by this.
>
> What tips or suggestions would you give to her caregiver/s to help Maeve in this stage?
>
> **Case study 3: Joe**
>
> Joe is four and is in stage 3 of Erikson's theory. Joe is adapting to a change in family structure following the arrival of his baby sister.
>
> What tips or suggestions would you give to his parents to help Joe in this stage?

John Bowlby

John Bowlby is best known for his theory of attachment (1969). Bowlby was a psychoanalyst who, like Sigmund Freud, believed that humans have an innate need to bond with their primary caregiver. Unlike Freud, he was not satisfied that the child's love for their mother/caregiver came from oral gratification.

Bowlby believed that bonding was based on a need for survival and that humans desired a 'safe haven' from which to explore the world. If there was consistent nurturing attachment from the mother or carer, an individual would develop into a more confident and well-adjusted person. Bowlby called this single strong attachment that happens from birth between a child and their mother/fundamental carer 'monotropy'. According to Bowlby, the first two and a half years of the child's life are critical for the bonding to happen and the attachment to be secure.

Bowlby was influenced by the work of Austrian zoologist Konrad Lorenz and his theory of imprinting, which posited that an animal forms an attachment to the first thing it sees. Observing newly hatched goslings, Lorenz discovered that they would follow the first moving object they saw – often Lorenz himself. Bowlby was also influenced by Harry Harlow's work with rhesus monkeys. (Further information on Harlow can be found in Chapter 7.)

Bowlby carried out significant research in the areas of attachment, child development and delinquent behaviour and spent much of his time working with children who exhibited challenging conduct. He became interested in how separation from caregivers impacted on a person in their future life, developing research which suggested that disruptions or lack of attachment between a mother/caregiver and child could lead to difficulties later with social, emotional, cognitive and holistic development.

Maternal Deprivation Theory (1944)

In the '44 Thieves' investigation, Bowlby studied 44 juveniles who had been referred to him for stealing. He used a control group of another 44 juveniles who had emotional problems but had not stolen. Of the 44 juveniles who had stolen, over 50 per cent of them had gone through a period of separation from their caregiver for more than six months during the first five years of their life. From the control group, only two had gone through separation. He also discovered that 32 per cent of the 'thieves' were not able to show affection or a caring attitude towards others and furthermore that most of these juveniles had spent prolonged periods of time away from their caregiver before the age of five. Bowlby concluded from his study that maternal deprivation in early childhood leads to emotional damage and possible antisocial behaviour later in life.

Focus on … John Bowlby (1907–1990)

Edward John Mostyn Bowlby was born in 1907 in London. His parents sent him away to boarding school at age seven, an experience he later described as traumatic. Bowlby studied psychology at Trinity College, Cambridge, and after graduation spent time working with children and delinquent young people. Going on to become a child psychiatrist, Bowlby was influenced by the work of psychoanalyst and play therapist Melanie Klein, though later became dissatisfied with her techniques when he concluded that they were based too much on fantasy. His development of attachment theory, though not without its critics, has been described as the dominant approach to understanding early social development and has given rise to many studies into the formation of children's close relationships.

Therapeutic Interventions in Psychoanalysis

Free Association

Free association is a technique whereby the client is asked to think and talk freely about whatever comes to mind as regards the situation, topic or person they are discussing in therapy. This process allows the person to verbalise anything that comes up in a safe and non-judgemental way. The therapist then attempts to establish if there are any patterns or clues in the content of the stream of thoughts shared by the client.

Dream Analysis

This is a practice whereby the client shares the content of their dreams and may be asked to keep a dream journal. The therapist and the client may start to see patterns or repetitions in the dreams. The therapist will analyse the dreams by looking at the contents and attributing various meanings to objects, people and places. Many therapists believe, as Freud did, that dreams hold symbolic meaning and that this symbolic meaning holds the key to uncovering what is being held in the person's unconscious mind.

Transference

Sometimes a client may express feelings towards the therapist or someone else in their life that appear to be based on the patient's past feelings about someone else. This is known as 'transference'. The client is usually unaware that they are doing this. Rather, they are trying to resolve an unconscious issue. Transference can be actively encouraged by the therapist as a therapeutic tool in an effort to understand a client's unconscious mental processes and comprehend their actions, behaviours and feelings. In all cases, a therapist should make the patient aware of when transference is happening.

Play Therapy and Art Therapy

There are several psychology perspectives that offer play and art therapy as interventions. In the psychoanalytic perspective the child will bring up unconscious issues via their play and so the therapist will focus on the symbols in the child's play as a way to reveal the deeper meaning of what is happening in the unconscious mind of the child. Art therapy is used in a similar way whereby the actual art or drawings themselves are studied to reveal deeper meanings, such as by observing the size, colour and shape of the objects in the drawing.

Criticisms of Psychoanalysis

Psychoanalysis has been heavily criticised for lacking a scientific basis. Early criticism levelled at Sigmund Freud related to his lack of quantitative data (Freud relied on case studies and anecdotes) and his theories have been criticised as overly simple. Freud has also been criticised for placing too much emphasis on sex as well as on childhood development, with the counterargument being that personality development is a lifelong process.

Jung's archetypes have been criticised as being 'mystical' and pseudoscientific, overly stereotyped and culturally biased. They are often studied more as historical artefact than as a major contribution to the science of the mind and behaviour.

Review what you have learned

1. Of what branch of psychoanalysis is Anna Freud considered the founder?
2. Name the four major Jungian archetypes.
3. In your own words, define the terms 'introvert' and 'extrovert'.
4. Name one of Erikson's eight stages of psychosocial development and explain it in your own words.
5. What theory is John Bowlby best known for?
6. Name and explain two therapeutic interventions in psychoanalysis.
7. Identify one criticism of the area of psychoanalysis.

chapter 4
THE BEHAVIOURIST PERSPECTIVE

IN THIS CHAPTER YOU WILL LEARN ABOUT:

+ the founders and principles of behaviourism
+ Ivan Pavlov, John B. Watson and classical conditioning
+ B.F. Skinner and operant conditioning
+ therapeutic interventions in behaviourism
+ criticisms of behaviourism.

What is Behaviourism?

The concept of behaviourism is based on the idea that all behaviours are acquired through conditioning, and conditioning occurs through interaction with the environment. In other words, our actions are shaped by our environment. The behaviourist approach introduced the scientific methods to psychology. Laboratory experiments were used and objective and measurable data was obtained. Popularised by the work of John B. Watson, early work in the field of behaviour was conducted by Russian physiologist Ivan Pavlov in his work on a form of learning behaviour called conditioned reflex.

Pavlov's Dog

Engaged in a research project to understand the process of digestion in dogs, Pavlov measured a number of factors, including how much a dog salivated when it was given food. During his research he discovered a phenomenon he called 'psychic salivation', whereby a dog would actually salivate before it was given food. Since Pavlov believed that digestion involved a series of reflexes, he set out to determine why the dogs exhibited this response. His discovery became the basis for what is now known as classical conditioning – the type of learning that happens unconsciously.

Focus on … Ivan Pavlov (1849–1936)

Ivan Petrovich Pavlov was born in Ryazan, Russia, in 1849. He initially began seminary studies, but changed to St Petersburg University, where he received his doctorate in physiology. After a few years spent in Germany, he became a professor at the Military Medical Academy in St Petersburg. His work on the digestive system, started in 1879, earned him the Nobel Prize in Physiology or Medicine in 1904. His work on classical conditioning would soon overshadow the research that had earned him this prize.

Classical Conditioning

Classical conditioning explores how an unconditioned stimulus in the environment can evoke an existing unconditioned (innate) response. In his experiment, Pavlov rang a bell right before a dog was given food. He continued to pair the sound of the bell with the presentation of food. After repeating this many times, the dog eventually began to associate the bell with food. When the bell was rung the dog would salivate as it was expecting to receive food. Therefore, even if the dog did not receive food when the bell was rung, it was conditioned to expect food at the sound of the bell. The food was the unconditioned stimulus and salivation was an unconditioned response.

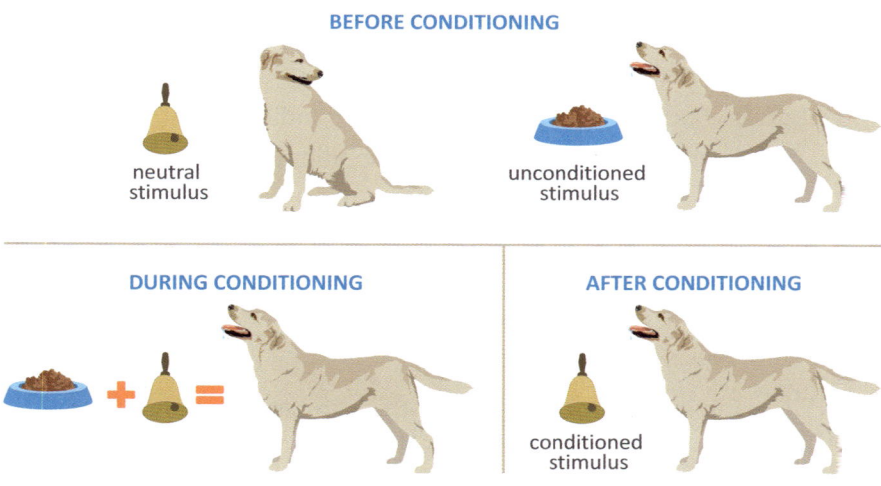

Here is a list of terms and definitions in relation to classical conditioning:

- **Unconditioned stimulus:** Something in the environment that causes an automatic response; for example, the smell of food when you are hungry would be an unconditioned stimulus.

- **Unconditioned response:** The automatic or unlearned reaction; for example, a response to the smell of food would be to salivate. Salivation in this case is the unconditioned response as it is not a learned response.

- **Neutral stimulus:** Something in the environment that does not cause a natural or automatic response on its own.

- **Conditioned stimulus:** A neutral stimulus that is paired with an unconditioned stimulus until it creates a response. For example, if the food is paired with a bell, then with repeated exposure to the food and bell, eventually the bell on its own will elicit the same response as the food. The bell is the conditioned stimulus.

- **Conditioned response:** A learned response that is usually the same as the unconditioned response; in this case the conditioned response would be salivation. However, salivation would happen when the bell rings without the need for food.

- **Generalisation:** The occurrence of a similar response to another similar stimulus.

- **Extinction:** The ending of the learned or conditioned response after a period of time when the unconditioned stimulus is no longer presented alongside the conditioned stimulus.

In summary:

- **Before conditioning:** A neutral stimulus does not naturally cause any response while an unconditioned stimulus causes an unconditioned response.

- **During conditioning:** The neutral stimulus is repeatedly paired with the unconditioned stimulus.

- **After conditioning:** The conditioned stimulus causes a conditioned response.

John B. Watson and the 'Little Albert' Experiment

The American psychologist John B. Watson developed the work of Pavlov by conducting experiments with humans. One of these experiments was the controversial 'Little Albert' study (1920). Working with a nine-month-old boy given the name 'Albert', he exposed the child to a number of stimuli, including a white rat, of which he showed no fear. Allowing Albert to play with the rat, Watson then made a loud noise every time Albert touched the rat, which would startle and upset the infant. After several such pairings of the two stimuli, Albert was then presented with just the rat, at which he would become very distressed and fearful. The child now associated the rat with the loud, upsetting noise. The rat, originally the neutral stimulus, had become a conditioned stimulus and it elicited an emotional response (conditioned response) similar to the distress (unconditioned response) originally caused by the noise (unconditioned stimulus).

> **Task**
>
> **Think-Pair-Share**
> Can you think of any examples of classical conditioning in action in your daily life? Can you think of any advertisements that utilise classical conditioning in the promotion of their products? What methods do they use? Pair and share your thoughts.

Focus on ... John B. Watson (1878–1958)

John Broadus Watson is known as the founder of behaviourism. Educated in a one-room schoolhouse on a farm, he would go on to complete his PhD at the University of Chicago. He studied under John Dewey and James Angell, two of the leaders of the functionalist approach. After completing his PhD, he started teaching at the University of Chicago. Four years later, he was offered a full professorship in psychology at Johns Hopkins University. In 1913 Watson began publishing a series that outlined his behaviourist approach. While at Johns Hopkins, he met graduate student Rosalie Rayner, who became his wife. After collaborating with Rayner on the 'Little Albert' experiment, Watson became interested in consumer behaviour. He took a job with the J. Walter Thompson advertising firm, becoming vice-president within four years. Watson not only founded an entire approach to psychology, but perhaps was also the first psychologist to utilise psychological theory in another field entirely.

B.F. Skinner and Operant Conditioning

The American behaviourist B.F. Skinner is regarded as the father of operant conditioning. His work was based on Edward Thorndike's law of effect (1898). Thorndike, an American psychologist, observed the behaviour of animals, usually cats, trying to escape from puzzle boxes in order to retrieve some fish. The law of effect states that if a certain behaviour is followed by a reward, that behaviour is more likely to reoccur. However, if a certain behaviour is followed by a punishment the behaviour is less likely to reoccur. Thorndike was very interested in how rewards and punishments could influence learning and went on to develop the three laws of learning. These laws have been used extensively in education and in the development of operant conditioning.

As a behaviourist and building on the work of Thorndike and his law of effect, Skinner (1948) believed that thoughts and motivations could not be used to explain behaviour. Instead, he said that we should focus only on the outer behaviour and patterns of a person. He developed the operant conditioning chamber, a piece of laboratory apparatus used to study animal behaviour, commonly known as the Skinner box.

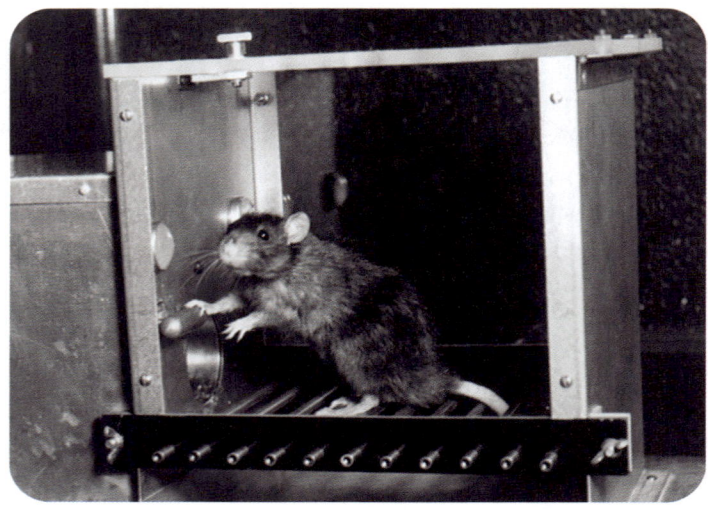

Focus on ... B.F. Skinner (1904–1990)

Burrhus Frederic Skinner was born in the small town of Susquehanna, Pennsylvania in 1904. As a child, he enjoyed building and inventing things. With ambitions to become a novelist, he completed a degree in English literature. However, he became disillusioned with his literary ability and instead pursued his interest in human behaviour. His encounter with Watson's behaviourism led him to study psychology, and he went on to develop his own version of behaviourism. He received his PhD from Harvard in 1931, and returned there in 1948 as professor, where he remained for the rest of his life.

The Skinner Box

Developed by Skinner while he was a graduate student at Harvard, the operant conditioning chamber is a box with a lever or a disc that, when pressed by the animal, would deliver food through an opening. Skinner observed that if the animal received food after pressing the lever, they were more likely to repeat the behaviour. Their behaviour was reinforced in a positive way and was therefore more likely to happen again. This is the basis of operant conditioning: a response that is followed by a reinforcing stimulus is more likely to happen again.

Four Consequences

Skinner identified four consequences that he believed shaped behaviour.

1. **Positive reinforcement:** Increases a specific behaviour by giving a reward or something enjoyable; for example, a student who completes all their homework receives a gold star.

2. **Negative reinforcement:** Increases a specific behaviour by removing something unpleasant; for example, a person who puts on sunscreen before going to the beach on a sunny day does not get sunburned.

3. **Positive punishment:** Decreases a behaviour by adding something unpleasant; for example, a child who does not clean their room is punished by having to clean the entire house at the weekend.

4. **Negative punishment:** Decreases a behaviour by taking something pleasant away; for example, a teenager who breaks curfew is punished by having their phone taken away for a period of time.

> **Task** **Think-Pair-Share**
> Operant conditioning is now used in many different ways in everyday life. Can you think of how operant conditioning might be used in a classroom setting? Pair and share your thoughts.

Therapeutic Interventions in Behaviourism

Aversive Conditioning

Aversive conditioning (aversion therapy) is used to help a person give up a behaviour by associating it with something unpleasant. For example, a coat of unpleasant-tasting varnish can be applied to nails to discourage nail-biting.

Exposure Therapy

Exposure therapy treats a client's fear or anxiety by exposing them to the object or situation that causes their anxiety with the idea being that they will eventually learn to cope with it. For example, someone with a fear of snakes might be instructed on how to handle a snake.

Systematic Desensitisation

Systematic desensitisation works by slowly exposing a client to a stimulus until a calm and pleasant state is associated with increasing levels of that stimulus. For example, if a client is afraid of spiders, they are first shown a spider in a glass cage. Next, they are presented with the spider while calm music is playing. Then, the spider is brought closer and the client is told to breathe deeply and try to associate the spider with pleasant, calming thoughts, until eventually the spider is next to them and the client is relaxed.

Criticisms of Behaviourism

One major criticism of behaviourism is that while it introduced the scientific method to psychology, many of the early experiments conducted were on animals, and so their results could not be readily applied to the human condition. As well as that, behaviourists do not take into account differing genetic or biological dispositions but rather think it is only the environment that determines how a person behaves. This is considered a very limited view that fails to deal with factors such as motivation, emotions and expectations.

Review what you have learned

1. Explain the concept of behaviourism in your own words.
2. What is classical conditioning? Explain it using one example.
3. List Skinner's four types of consequence.
4. Explain exposure therapy and give an example.
5. Identify two limitations of the behaviourist perspective.

chapter 5
HUMANISTIC PSYCHOLOGY

IN THIS CHAPTER YOU WILL LEARN ABOUT:

- the founders and principles of humanistic psychology
- Abraham Maslow's Hierarchy of Needs
- Carl Rogers and client-centred therapy
- therapeutic interventions in humanist psychology
- criticisms of humanistic psychology.

Humanism – the 'Third Force'

While developments in psychology were taking place in Europe, other developments were taking place in the USA. Sometimes referred to as the 'third force' in psychology, after psychoanalysis and behaviourism, humanism was developed by Abraham Maslow. Maslow believed that Freud and Skinner were overly negative in their approaches to psychology and so set out to develop a more positive approach to the aspects of human nature.

Maslow was heavily influenced by Gestalt psychologist Max Wertheimer. Gestalt theory emphasised that the whole of anything is greater than its parts. Like Wilhelm Wundt, the founder of structuralism, Wertheimer studied perception and sensation. However, unlike structuralism, which broke things down into smaller parts, Wertheimer's focus was on things as a whole.

Maslow was in favour of this holistic approach to dealing with a person and their unique situation. He became very well known for his hierarchy of needs, self-actualisation and peak experiences. These concepts formed the groundwork for the school of humanism, which has had a resurgence in recent years because of the growth of popular psychology.

Focus on ... Abraham Maslow (1908–1970)

Abraham Maslow was born in 1908 in Brooklyn, New York, the first of seven children. His parents had emigrated from Russia and he was raised in the Jewish faith. His father hoped that he would pursue law, but instead Abraham studied psychology at the University of Wisconsin, where his doctoral adviser was Harry Harlow. He became head of the psychology department at the University of Brandeis in Massachusetts and stayed there until 1969. He is best known for his work on humanism and the hierarchy of needs.

Maslow's Hierarchy of Needs

The theory of hierarchy of needs (1943) arose from Maslow's attempt to answer the question of what motivates human behaviour. Maslow believed that human beings were motivated by a set of needs and that they would work on attaining these needs in a certain order. There were five levels of needs in the hierarchy.

PSYCHOLOGY: AN INTRODUCTION

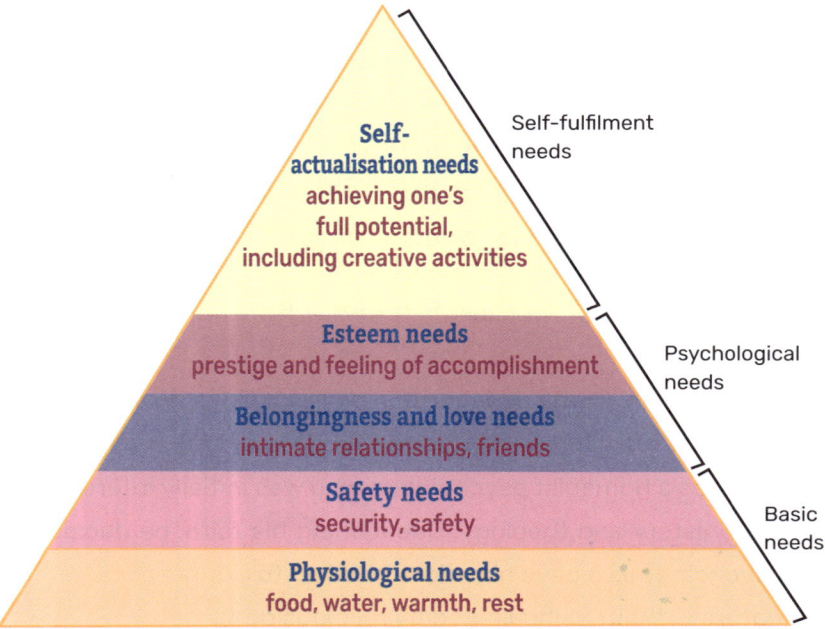

1. At the first level, the individual seeks to meet basic physiological needs such as food, water, shelter and clothing.

2. When these basic needs are met, the individual can move to fulfil the need for safety and security in the forms of shelter and employment.

3. The third need concerns love and belonging, wherein the individual seeks to fulfil social needs with a focus on finding a romantic partner, friendships, family and a place in the community.

4. After these needs are attained, the individual is able to move to the fourth level, which is based on esteem. Here the individual strives for success and acknowledgement of their achievements and efforts, for example through work or sport. The individual seeks to make a contribution to and feel valued by society.

5   Finally, at the peak of the hierarchy is the need for self-actualisation. Maslow believed that every human being has a need to fulfil their highest potential. If every other need is met, an individual can attend to their own personal growth and develop their gifts and talents, for the benefit of themselves, those around them and society at large.

Carl Rogers and Client-Centred Therapy

Unlike behaviourism, humanistic psychology examines how one views oneself and how one works through the process of self-actualisation. Carl Rogers was a humanist psychologist who was initially interested in the fields of history and theology. Questioning his faith, he decided to pursue psychology as it gave him more freedom to explore and examine human nature without being limited by religious doctrine.

Rogers maintained that each person has a unique sense of self and a great deal of control over how they live their lives and the goals and dreams they have. Each person, according to Rogers, has an innate need to grow and develop, and this is what guides a person's behaviour. Humanist theory believes that behaviour comes directly from an individual's own feelings about and perceptions of themselves and is not motivated by the outside world.

Rogers believed that a person develops a self-concept early on in life and that this self-concept is influenced by parental involvement with the child. If a child receives love and affection from the parent, the child will be more likely to develop a healthy self-concept. If a child has to work for love and affection from the parent, the child may develop low self-esteem.

Rogers worked with his clients in a facilitative way, and in contrast to other theorists did not believe that the therapist was the director of the sessions. He believed that a therapist must demonstrate unconditional positive regard for their client, showing respect for the client as a human being whether or not they agreed with their client's actions, and being empathetic and non-judgemental, validating the client's feelings at all times. This, he felt, would help strengthen and increase the client's self-worth and self-esteem. He termed this approach 'client-centred therapy' (1959).

Focus on … Carl Rogers (1902–1987)

Carl Rogers was born in Illinois in 1902, the fourth of six children. He performed very well in school, reading at a young age and skipping some grades. In 1919 he enrolled at the University of Wisconsin to study agriculture. He switched his focus to history, then to religion, before settling on psychology. He enrolled in a clinical psychology programme in Columbia University and received his doctorate from there in 1931. Rogers wrote numerous books and articles on humanist theory and is best known for his client-centred therapy approach. He was nominated for a Nobel Peace Prize in 1987 for his work in conflict resolution in Northern Ireland and South Africa.

Task **Think-Pair-Share**
According to Rogers (1959), the term 'self-concept' was made up of three parts. What do you think these parts are? Think about it, then pair and share your opinions.

Rogers' Theory of Self-Concept

Rogers theorised that a conception of self was made up of three parts:

1. **Self-image:** This is how you see yourself, including how you look physically and how you act. For example: Lucy is 17 years old. She is 5 feet 4 inches tall, with brown hair and brown eyes. She would describe herself as bubbly.

2. **Ideal self:** This is how you would like to see yourself or the person you would like to be. For example: Lucy would like it if she were taller, and she would like to be seen as more serious and less bubbly.

3. **Self-esteem:** This is how much you like, accept and value yourself and can be based on how you feel others view you as well as on the comparison you make of yourself to others. For example: Lucy is generally comfortable with herself but sometimes compares herself to her best friend, who she believes is more popular, which can lead to feelings of inadequacy. Overall, however, she feels loved and supported by her family and friends.

REFLECT

What is your self-concept? Fill in the table.

Self-image – how do you see yourself?	
Ideal self – what is your ideal self?	
Self-esteem – do you like, accept and value yourself, refraining from comparisons to others?	

Congruence and Incongruence (1959)

Rogers believed that if a person's self-image and ideal self were in alignment, that person was in a state of congruence and would experience high levels of esteem and self-regard. However, if a person's self-image and ideal self were not in alignment, with large gaps between the two states, a person would be in a state of incongruence, leading to negative or low self-esteem. He felt that a child in receipt of unconditional positive regard in the form of unconditional love and affection was more likely to become a fully functioning person who is congruent and able to work towards self-actualisation.

Therapeutic Interventions in Humanistic Psychology

Person-centred Therapy

Rogerian or person-centred therapy revolves solely around the person first and not their problems. The person is viewed as an expert in their own life and the therapist is there to listen, facilitate and validate the client. Rogers believed that, as an acorn becomes an oak, every person works towards becoming a fully functional person with a desire to reach full potential. Each person will strive towards actualisation. This actualisation tendency, according to Rogers, was an innate desire in all human beings. The main technique used in person-centred therapy is reflection, whereby the therapist repeats to the client what they have said. This allows the client to see and understand themselves more clearly. The therapist interacts with the client in a non-judgemental way and gives them unconditional positive regard, treating them with great care and empathy and thus truly allowing them to explore their deepest feelings, dreams and desires in a safe, supportive space.

Transpersonal Therapy

Transpersonal therapy focuses on the health of the person's spirit. It emphasises a person's spiritual path or spiritual enlightenment, with the aim being that the person gain a full understanding of themselves, their relationships and their capabilities.

> **REFLECT**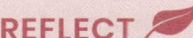
>
> What spiritual traditions can you identify in your culture? What are the benefits of these traditions?

Play Therapy

Play therapy came from the perspectives of both psychoanalysis and humanistic psychology. In play therapy the child has a safe space in which to explore their feelings and work through patterns or traumas that need to be addressed through specific play activities. The therapist provides support and encouragement for the child to reveal what is going on. In humanistic play therapy the child themselves directs the activities and the play that they want to engage in and the therapist offers validation and support to the child.

Mindfulness

Mindfulness has been part of humanistic psychology from the beginning. Over the years, mindfulness has become a much larger field in the area of psychology. At a basic level, it is the practice of being fully aware of what is happening in the present moment. This can be done by using the breath as an anchor or by tuning in to the senses. There are many different practices that help a client deal only with the present moment in an attempt to decrease mind chatter, worry and anxiety.

Criticisms of Humanistic Psychology

Many theorists argue that humanistic psychology is too subjective and tries to encapsulate things which are unquantifiable, such as self-actualisation. Some theorists also believe that terms such as 'self-actualisation' are too vague.

Review what you have learned

1. Explain Maslow's Hierarchy of Needs.
2. Explain Rogers' concept of client-centred therapy.
3. Explain Rogers' concept of congruence and incongruence.
4. What is the aim of transpersonal therapy?

chapter 6
THE COGNITIVE PERSPECTIVE

IN THIS CHAPTER YOU WILL LEARN ABOUT:

- the founders and principles of cognitive psychology
- Jean Piaget and cognitive development
- Albert Ellis and REBT
- Aaron Beck and cognitive therapy
- Lev Vygotsky and sociocultural theory
- therapeutic interventions in cognitive psychology
- criticisms of cognitive psychology.

What is Cognitive Psychology?

Cognitive psychology is a school of thought that examines the mental processes of attention, memory, problem solving, learning and intelligence. It could be argued that the work of Wilhelm Wundt on perception and William James on introspection were the beginnings of cognitive psychology. Whereas behaviourism looked at the actions of people based on external environmental influences, cognitive psychology sought to examine the mental thought process that alters a person's behaviour.

Jean Piaget and Theory of Cognitive Development

Jean Piaget's theory of cognitive development (1936) concerns the nature and development of human intelligence. It deals with how humans come to acquire, construct and use knowledge. Piaget was a nature theorist. Studying children and their intelligence tests, he proposed that children were born with a basic mental structure that was genetic and on which all learning and knowledge was based. Piaget believed that this was universal for all children and not determined by the environment. This theory became known worldwide, especially in the fields of child development and education.

Focus on … Jean Piaget (1896–1980)

Jean Piaget was born in 1896 in Switzerland. From a young age he showed an interest in the natural sciences. He obtained a PhD in Zoology from the University of Neuchatel, Switzerland, in 1918. Piaget observed his own children, which served as the basis for many of his theories in child development. Best known for his work on schemas and his four-stage theory of cognitive development, Piaget developed the idea that children think differently to adults and progress in their intellectual capacity as they mature.

According to Piaget, the four stages of cognitive development are:

1 the sensorimotor stage (birth to two years)

2 the preoperational stage (ages two to seven)

3 the concrete operational stage (ages seven to 11)

4 the formal operational stage (ages 12 and up).

For Piaget, children were like little scientists, taking in information and playing an active role in their own learning. As they interact with the world, they add to their knowledge, build upon existing knowledge and adapt previously held ideas to accommodate new ideas.

Schema, Assimilation and Accommodation

To understand Piaget's four stages of cognitive development, first we need to understand Piaget's concepts of schema, assimilation and accommodation.

Schema

A schema is a category of knowledge that helps us to understand and interpret the world. Think of it as a folder in the brain. When we encounter new information, we store it away in a folder. When we encounter similar information, we can add it to this folder. As experience happens, we can use it to add to or modify previously existing folders, or schema, or create new schema altogether.

For example, when a child first encounters a piece of fruit, say a banana, they might question what it is with their caregiver, who will tell them, and they might taste the fruit. Thus they create a schema for fruit based on this experience of a banana and the knowledge they have acquired.

Assimilation

Now suppose the child is introduced to a peach. They are told by their caregiver that it is also a fruit, and they may taste it. The child will take in this information and modify previously existing information to include this new observation of what fruit is. This process of taking in new or similar information into our already existing schema is known as assimilation. It is a somewhat subjective process because of the tendency to try and modify new information to fit in with already existing beliefs.

Accommodation

More adaptation and restructuring of the folder, or schema, occurs when the child encounters new information. New folders might be created altogether. This is the process of accommodation. For example, suppose the child now encounters a pepper. They will attempt to assimilate this new information into their 'fruit' schema. However, upon being told that it is a vegetable and having perhaps tasted it, the child will need to create a new schema for vegetable as well as modify their existing schema for fruit to accommodate what it is not.

Equilibrium and Disequilibrium

Alongside these concepts of schema, assimilation and association, Piaget believed that we lived our lives in a process of equilibrium and disequilibrium. As we go through life, we learn new things. When we have to learn new information, it might be an uncomfortable process. We are in a state of disequilibrium. When we have assimilated or accommodated the new information successfully, we return to a state of equilibrium.

The Four Stages of Cognitive Development

Sensorimotor stage (0–2 years)	Preoperational stage (2–7 years)	Concrete operational stage (7–11 years)	Formal operational stage (12 years and over)
The child engages with their surroundings by using their senses, experiencing the world through touch, taste, smell, sight and hearing.	The child engages in pretend and symbolic play. They do not understand operations or logical thought and still tend to think of things in concrete terms. The features of this stage are:	The child starts to understand operations and logical thought. The features of this stage include:	The child can understand abstract thinking. The features of this stage include: ✚ Metacognition: the ability to think our own thoughts and processes

Sensorimotor stage (0–2 years)	Preoperational stage (2–7 years)	Concrete operational stage (7–11 years)	Formal operational stage (12 years and over)
The key feature of this stage is object permanence. At around eight months an infant understands the concept of object permanence: an object still exists even when out of sight. Prior to this, once an object was out of sight, it was out of mind.	✚ Animism: the belief that inanimate objects like teddy bears and dolls are alive and have feelings and a purpose ✚ Centration: focusing only on one element of a situation ✚ Egocentrism: not being able to see something from another person's point of view ✚ Symbolic play: role playing and pretending to be adults in play ✚ Irreversibility: the inability to understand that actions can be reversed	✚ Conservation: the ability to understand that solids and liquids do not change even if their appearance does ✚ Classification: the ability to organise items by identifying common features or traits ✚ Seriation: the ability to put things in a specific order based on quantifiable measures like height ✚ Reversibility: the understanding that steps in a process or action can be reversed	✚ Proportional reasoning: the ability to understand proportions like fractions ✚ Hypothetical reasoning: the ability to think about situations that may or may not take place but have not yet happened and may not happen

Cognitive Behavioural Therapy

Cognitive behavioural therapy (CBT) is an umbrella term for a group of many different therapies that share common elements. The first forms of CBT were rational emotive behavioural therapy (REBT) and cognitive therapy.

Albert Ellis and REBT

Albert Ellis (1955) initially studied psychoanalysis, but came to believe that rather than it being the unconscious thoughts and feelings that were causing people problems, it was conscious irrational assumptions that people made that caused them pain and suffering. The goal of REBT is to change irrational assumptions and beliefs into more rational ones.

Within REBT, Ellis created the ABC technique as a way for people to analyse the process of their thinking and break down how they may be creating or have created irrational assumptions or beliefs.

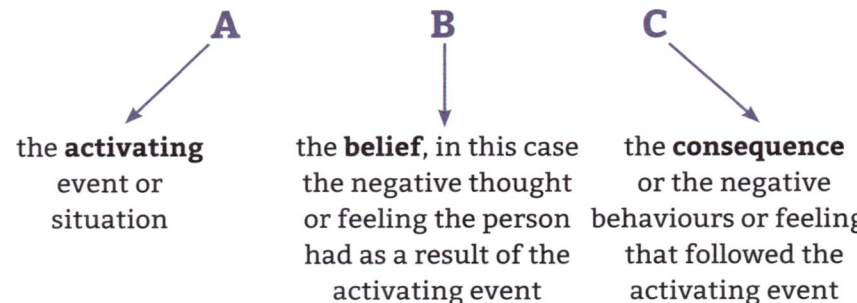

A	B	C
the **activating** event or situation	the **belief**, in this case the negative thought or feeling the person had as a result of the activating event	the **consequence** or the negative behaviours or feelings that followed the activating event

Let's look at an example.

> Today during the football match, Thomas missed an opportunity to score a goal. The other team scored two goals and Thomas's team scored none. After the match, Thomas felt that he was a failure and not good enough to be on the team. He was very upset for the entire evening and would not leave his bedroom, had no dinner and spoke to no one in the house.

- **A** The activating event was Thomas not scoring the goal.
- **B** The belief was that he was a failure.
- **C** The consequence was that Thomas was very upset for many hours and maybe even for many days later.

Here an REBT therapist would help Thomas to reframe his belief about himself, allowing him to change his assumption and know that he is not a failure if he does not succeed in everything he does, and that while winning is enjoyable, our self-worth does not derive from always winning/being perfect/constant achievement.

> ### Focus on ... Albert Ellis (1913–2007)
>
> Albert Ellis was born in 1913 and grew up in the Bronx, New York. The eldest of three children, he took on the role of being parent owing to his father often being away on business and his mother suffering from bipolar disorder. Earning a PhD in Clinical Psychology in 1947 from Columbia University, from the late 1940s onwards Ellis worked on REBT and began to call himself a rational therapist. He founded the Institute for Rational Living as a training institute and psychological clinic, today known as the Albert Ellis Institute. In a 1982 professional survey he was ranked the second-most influential psychotherapist in history, after Carl Rogers and before Sigmund Freud. Ellis died in 2007.

Aaron Beck and Cognitive Therapy

Aaron Beck (1967) also worked in the area of CBT and developed significant work on the subject of depression. In his work Beck came up with the following concepts.

- **The cognitive triad:** three negative forms of thinking that, according to Beck, people suffering from depression usually exhibit:

- negative view of the self
- negative view of the world
- negative view of the future.

+ These negative views impair normal cognitive processing and affect problem solving, memory and perception, leading a person to have an overall negative mindset.

+ **Negative self-schemas:** Beck believed that depression-prone people had negative schemas or beliefs about themselves. He said that these beliefs may have started in childhood if the person experienced traumatic events, such as criticism from a parent or carer, bullying or the death of a loved one.

+ **Cognitive distortions:** in other words, disordered thinking that displayed errors in logic.

Focus on ... Aaron Beck (1921–2021)

Aaron Temkin Beck was born in 1921 in Providence, Rhode Island. The youngest of five children, he attended Brown University and graduated with a degree in political science. After that he attended Yale and became a doctor. He studied psychoanalysis for some time and practised it as well, being very interested in treatments for depression. Eventually, Beck concluded that psychoanalysis did not hold the answers nor provide the treatments needed to treat depression so he switched to the cognitive approach, developing cognitive therapy. Cognitive behaviour therapy is now widely used in various settings, from education to counselling. Beck died in 2021, aged 100.

Cognitive Distortions

Regarding Beck's concept of cognitive distortions, sometimes our interpretation of events and their details can be inaccurate. The mind can be faulty or lead us to believe things that are simply not true. This happens to everyone occasionally and most people move on from this temporary form of usually negative thinking. However, for some people cognitive distortions become a pattern or way of thinking that can interfere with how they see life and interact with others. This inaccurate thinking can lead to increased stress, anxiety and other problems.

Here are some well-known cognitive distortions and examples.

- **Jumping to conclusions:** Not having all the evidence but assuming the worst.
  For example: In the morning when you enter the office, you say hello to your co-worker but he doesn't respond. You go to your desk thinking that he is upset with you. You mull over it, trying to establish what it is you have done to annoy him. Later in the day, you find out that he was preoccupied and worried about a family issue and didn't notice you this morning when you came in.

- **Over-generalising:** Taking one event that didn't work out as evidence that things never work out.
  For example: You do an interview but you do not get the job. You do not apply for any other job as you believe that no interview ever goes right for you and you will never get a job.

- **Black-and-white (all-or-nothing) thinking:** Where if a situation is not exactly as a person plans, they view it as being a failure.
  For example: You undertake a new lifestyle plan on 1 January, but on 4 January you miss your exercise session and as a result decide that the plan has been a failure and therefore discontinue it.

- **Catastrophising:** Expecting the worst to happen in a situation.
  For example: Your boss asks you to meet with her in her office for a chat and you come to the conclusion that you are being fired.

- **Personalisation:** Believing that you are responsible for events in a situation even if those events are not completely within your control.
  For example: A few of your students fail an exam you set, for which you blame yourself, despite the fact that there are many reasons why they may have failed as well as the fact that many others passed.

- **'Should' statements:** Using 'should' statements in relation to yourself or others, especially in your expectations of yourself or others, causing feelings of anger, guilt and frustration.
  For example: You fail your driving test, but tell yourself that you should have passed it, and that the driving instructor should not have failed you.

> **REFLECT**
>
> Think of a time when you might have engaged in one of these cognitive distortions. Was your thinking logical or rational? Were your beliefs borne out by reality?

Beck believed that if a person can become aware of their negative thinking, they can interrupt it and reframe it, thus changing their interpretations into more positive or at least more neutral ones. Cognitive therapy therefore helps people to develop alternative ways of thinking and behaving by challenging habitual negative patterns, thus leading to a healthier mindset.

Apply your learning

Research and identify three more types of cognitive distortions, giving examples for each.

Lev Vygotsky and Sociocultural Theory

In contrast to Jean Piaget, Lev Vygotsky was a nurture theorist. Vygotsky believed that children learn by watching more knowledgeable peers or family members and from social interactions within their environment. He was also very interested in how culture was passed on through generations and how customs, beliefs and traditions shaped social learning and interaction.

Zone of Proximal Development (ZPD)

Vygotsky theorised that everyone had a zone through which they could move to reach their potential. This zone was the space between someone's current knowledge and the knowledge they could obtain from a 'more knowledgeable other' (MKO). If someone attempts to move beyond this zone without help, support or scaffolding from an MKO, it would lead to frustration, resulting in barriers to further learning.

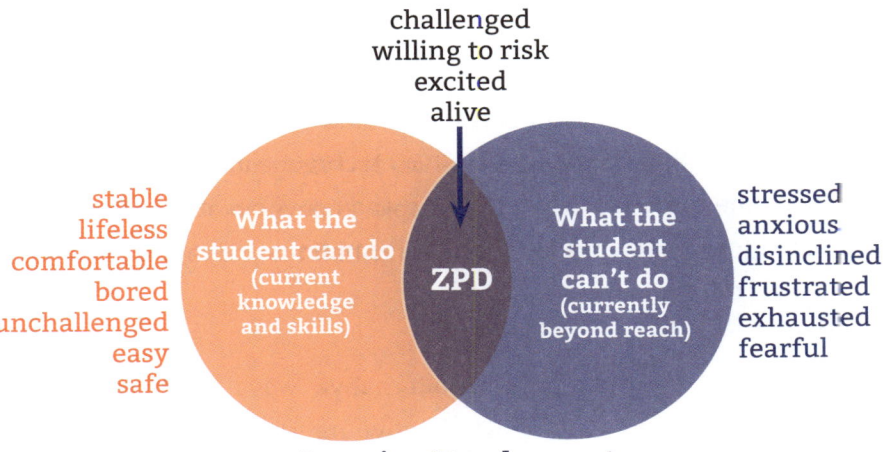

ZPD is the gap between what the student is currently capable of doing independently, and what they can do without support

Focus on … Lev Vygotsky (1896–1934)

Lev Vygotsky was born in Russia in 1896. He studied medicine and then law at Moscow University, but was more interested in the arts and history. In 1925 he completed a dissertation on the psychology of art, but was sick with tuberculosis for over a year. After his illness he studied memory, language, attention and learning. Vygotsky is best known for his work on the ZPD and sociocultural theory. He died of TB in 1934 at the age of 37.

Therapeutic Interventions in Cognitive Psychology

Rational Emotive Behavioural Therapy

The goal of REBT is to change irrational assumptions and beliefs into more rational ones. Ellis created the ABC technique as a way for people to analyse the process of their thinking and break down how they may be creating or have created irrational assumptions or beliefs.

Cognitive Behavioural Therapy

CBT helps the client to develop alternative ways of thinking and behaving by challenging habitual negative patterns such as negative thinking or assumptions, helping to form healthier thought patterns. This aims to reduce the client's distress and improve their quality of life.

Criticisms of Cognitive Psychology

One criticism levelled at the cognitive approach is that it can't be observed directly, meaning that we cannot see what is going on inside the brain of a person. Another criticism is that it does not take into account other influences on a person such as the environment in which they live and operate, their genetics, etc. A specific criticism made of the work of Piaget regarded the fact that most of his observations were made in relation to his own children or those of friends, as well as his theorising that stages were universal and unaffected by environmental factors.

Review what you have learned

1. List the four stages of cognitive development, according to Piaget.
2. What do the initials 'CBT' and 'REBT' stand for?
3. Explain the ABC model and name the theorist with whom it is associated.
4. Describe the cognitive triad and name the theorist with whom it is associated.
5. List and explain three cognitive distortions.
6. Explain the zone of proximal development in your own words.
7. Compare and contrast the approaches of Jean Piaget and Lev Vygotsky in the area of child development.

chapter 7

THE BIOLOGICAL PERSPECTIVE

IN THIS CHAPTER YOU WILL LEARN ABOUT:

- biological psychology
- the human nervous system
- the endocrine system
- biological evolution
- genetic psychology
- therapeutic interventions in biological psychology
- criticisms of biological psychology.

What is Biological Psychology?

Also known as physiological psychology, biological psychology is the study of the biology of behaviour. It focuses on the nervous system, hormones and genetics and examines the relationship between the mind and body, neural mechanisms and the influence of heredity on behaviour. Examining behaviours such as addiction from multiple perspectives, including the biological perspective, is seen as a more holistic approach to understanding why the behaviour is present.

The Human Nervous System

The nervous system is the command centre of the human body. It is a complex system divided into two parts: the central nervous system and the peripheral nervous system. Each system is made up of many neurons or nerve cells – the fundamental units of the brain and nervous system – which receive sensory input from the external world, send motor commands to our muscles and transform and relay electrical signals at every step in between. Each neuron is covered in a layer of insulation called myelin. The myelin protects the neuron and also helps with the smooth input or output of messages.

Different types of neurons have different jobs. Motor neurons are responsible for sending signals to the muscles for the body to move. Sensory neurons gather information from the senses and send it to the brain. Other neurons are responsible for automatic responses such as breathing and blinking.

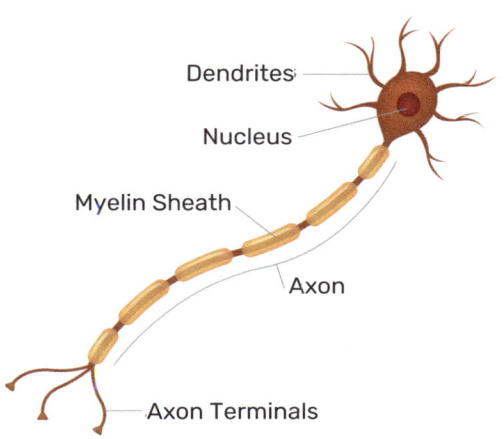

Neurotransmitters are chemicals present inside each neuron. Neurons do not touch each other; rather, at the end of each neuron there is a space known as a synapse. In order for two neurons to communicate with each other, one neuron sends neuro-transmitters into the synapse, which travel rapidly across the synapse into the next neuron.

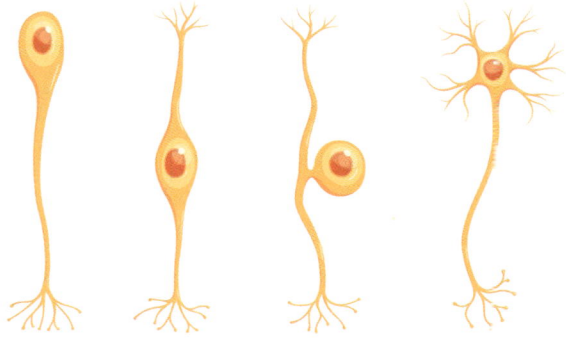

Important neurotransmitters studied in biological psychology include the following:

- **Dopamine:** Dopamine is one of the most extensively studied neurotransmitters in the field of genetic and biological psychology. Often called the pleasure chemical, it plays an extensive role in the areas of reward and pleasure. It is also involved in motivation and decision-making. Dopamine seems to have a role in addictive behaviour, attention deficit hyperactivity disorder (ADHD), schizophrenia, bipolar disorder and other disorders. It can be found in foods such as turkey and beef, dairy and eggs, bananas and dark chocolate, and is also produced during exercise, listening to music, meditation and being out in natural sunlight.

- **Serotonin:** Serotonin is involved in mood regulation and is often called the calming chemical. A lack of it has been related to depression and other abnormal disorders. Serotonin can be found in certain foods such as salmon, nuts and seeds, poultry, eggs and pineapple. It is also released in the body after exercising or being out in the sun.

- **Norepinephrine:** Norepinephrine is both a hormone and a neurotransmitter. It plays a role in memory, mood and stress levels and can be produced naturally by exercising, listening to music, meditation and regular sleep.

- **Glutamate:** Glutamate is classified as an excitatory neurotransmitter, meaning that it excites or stimulates nerve cells in order for them to receive important messages. Glutamate has to be carefully regulated as too much or too little can cause problems: too much can lead to restlessness and anxiety; too little can increase sleep problems and lower energy. Glutamate plays a role in sleep, pain transmission, concentration and learning. Foods that contain glutamate include tomatoes, mushrooms, cheese, meat and fish.

+ **Acetylcholine:** The first neurotransmitter to be discovered, acetylcholine is involved in regulating movement in the body. It is also involved in directing a person's attention and working memory. There are no foods or supplements that directly contain acetylcholine but the nutrient choline helps to make acetylcholine in the body. Foods that contain choline include meat, fish, eggs and wholegrain foods.

The Central Nervous System

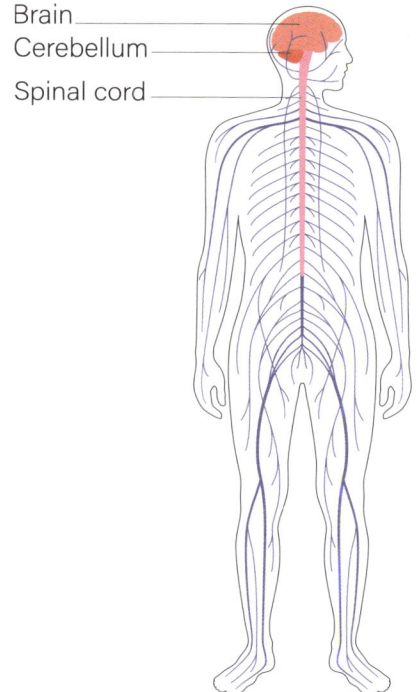

The central nervous system consists of the brain and the spinal cord. It is protected by three different layers or membranes called meninges. It is also covered in bone, the skull, the vertebrae and cerebrospinal fluid. Damage to the brain or the spinal cord can have severe consequences on the human body and mind. The brain is the chief organ of the nervous system, responsible for sending and receiving billions of messages throughout the body and processing information within seconds.

The Brain

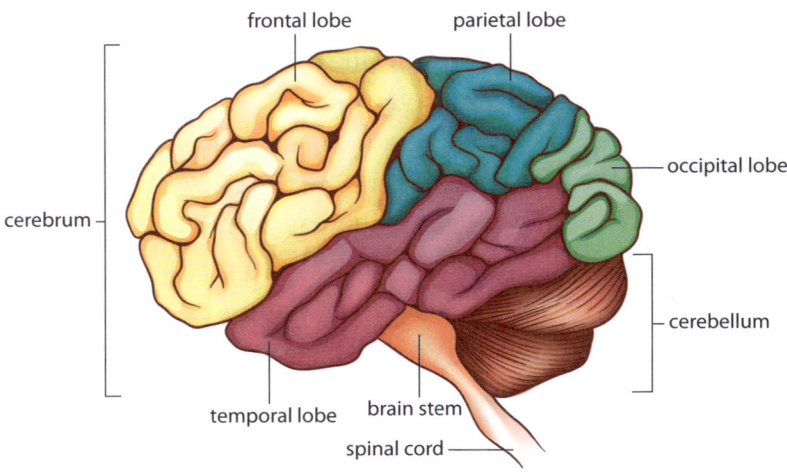

The brain consists of the cerebrum, the cerebellum and the brainstem.

- **The cerebrum:** This is the largest part of the brain and is responsible for complex processes such as the processing of sensory information, language formation and production, emotion, movement and cognitive processes. The brain is made up of an outer layer of cerebrum called the cerebral cortex, which looks wrinkled in appearance. This cortex is divided into the left and right cerebral hemispheres, which are joined by the corpus callosum. The corpus callosum allows both hemispheres to communicate with each other, and both sides of the brain work together in order for a person to function.

- **The cerebellum:** This is situated under the cerebrum and is responsible for coordination and balance.

- **The brainstem:** This connects the cerebrum and cerebellum to the spinal cord. It is involved in many automatic functions like breathing, regulation of temperature, blinking and coughing.

Lobes of the Brain

Each hemisphere has four interconnected lobes. Each lobe governs certain functions as well as working with the other lobes to enable a variety of functions.

1. **The frontal lobes:** These two lobes are the largest and sit at the front of the brain, directly behind the forehead. They are involved in movement, language, memory, behaviour and judgement. These lobes are considered to be responsible for our personality. Because of their location, they are often the parts of the brain damaged in accidents.

   Broca's area (named after French surgeon Paul Broca, who discovered it in 1861) is located in the frontal lobe of the brain and is involved in speech production. It is connected to Wernicke's area (a region of the brain involved in the comprehension of speech; see below) by a neuronal tract. It is also involved in language comprehension and in motor and sensorimotor integration.

> **THE AMERICAN CROWBAR CASE 1848**
>
> Phineas Gage was an American railroad foreman who suffered a major brain injury when an explosion in a tunnel caused an iron rod to penetrate his left frontal lobe. Miraculously, Gage survived. However, although his speech, movement and memory were unimpaired, his personality seemed to change, with co-workers stating that he was not the same, becoming unreliable and showing a disrespect towards them. Little, however, was documented about his personality changes after the accident. Gage died 12 years later of epileptic seizures. His skull and the iron rod were put on display at the Harvard Medical School's museum in Cambridge, Massachusetts.

2. **The temporal lobes:** These two lobes are the second largest lobes and sit behind the ears. They are involved in the processing of sound from the ears as well as the area of speech production and fluency. The temporal lobes are also part of the limbic system (see below). These lobes work with the limbic system in the areas of learning, memory and other automatic functions such as appetite and sexual arousal.

   Wernicke's area (discovered by German neurologist Carl Wernicke in 1874) is located in the temporal lobe and is a key area in the understanding of speech. It is close to the auditory cortex in the brain and is believed to have a very important role in the comprehension of speech sounds and language comprehension.

3. **The parietal lobes:** These two lobes are located behind the frontal lobes and on top of the temporal lobes. They are involved in sensory processing in the body and integrate information about touch, location and position in space, temperature and pain. They also play a role in language processing.

4. **The occipital lobes:** These two lobes are located at the back of the head and are involved in visual perception. This includes the identification of colours, objects, reading and writing and the ability to see objects in motion.

Other important structures in the brain include the following:

- **The hypothalamus:** A small structure located at the base of the brain near the brainstem and pituitary gland and made up of three different regions, the hypothalamus is involved in controlling appetite, hormone secretion and production. It is the link between the endocrine and nervous systems in the body. It also regulates other processes such as body temperature, emotions and other physiological cycles.

- **The pituitary gland:** Known as the master gland in the body, the pituitary gland works in conjunction with the hypothalamus, together forming the neuroendocrine system. They work with the other glands and organs in the body to closely monitor the production and secretion of various hormones responsible for vital and critical functions such as growth, repair, digestion, reproduction and so on.

- **The pineal gland:** The main function of the pineal gland is to secrete melatonin, which helps to regulate the sleep cycles in the body.

- **The thalamus:** The thalamus is often known as a relay centre. It interprets sensory information that comes and goes to the cortex. It also plays a role in memory, motor activity and emotion. There are two thalami in the brain, one in each hemisphere.

- **The basal ganglia:** This is a group of nuclei that work together for motor control and also play a role in habit formation, reward, reinforcement and addictive behaviours.

- **The limbic system:** This is a primal part of the brain involved in emotional and behavioural responses. It is made up of the hippocampus and amygdala. The hippocampus comes as a pair (like many other structures in the brain). It is the memory centre, helping to connect sensory information with memories. The amygdala plays a role in emotional responses and also connects emotion with memories. The stronger an emotional response to an event, the stronger a memory will be. The hypothalamus, thalamus and basal ganglia are also involved in the functions of the limbic system.

The Peripheral Nervous System

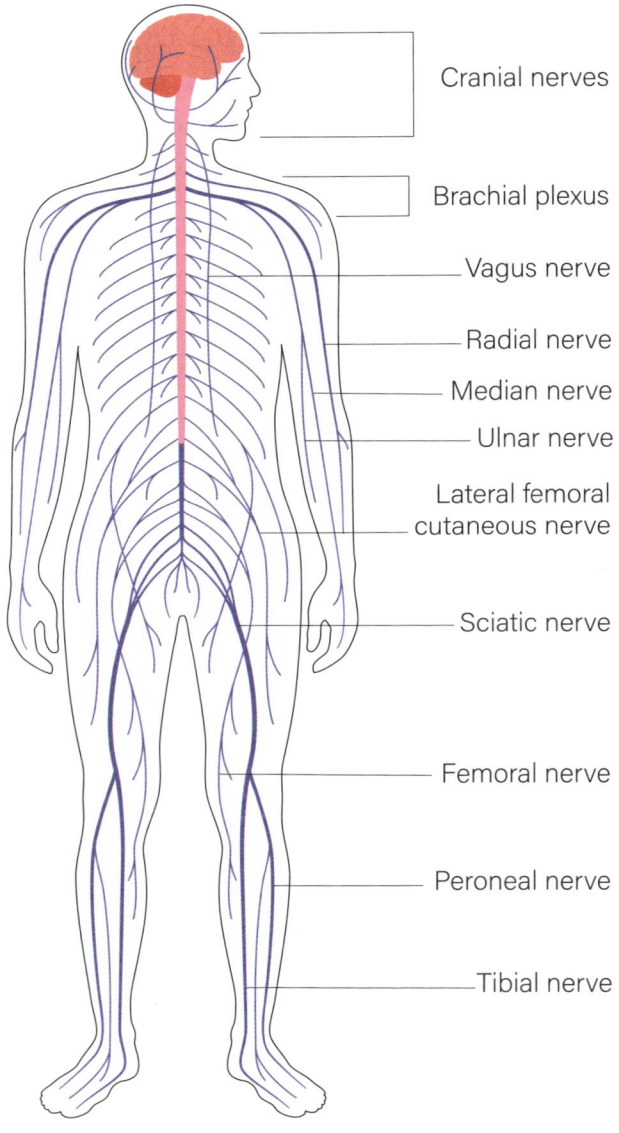

Unlike the central nervous system, which is protected by different layers, the peripheral nervous system is not protected by bone and can therefore be more easily damaged than the brain and spinal cord. If the central nervous system is the power hub of the body, the peripheral nervous system is the cables that bring that power to the rest of the body so that the organs and muscles can function. It is made up of different types of nerve cells, which send messages to and from the central nervous system. Motor neurons, as we learned, are involved in movement, while sensory neurons are involved in sensory processing. The peripheral nervous system can be subdivided into three different systems:

1. **The somatic nervous system:** Often called the voluntary nervous system, it contains nerve cells for the senses and for movement and is responsible for sending messages to and away from the brain and spinal cord. These messages inform the central nervous system about sensory information and about voluntary movements such as walking, running and carrying things.

2. **The autonomic nervous system:** This system regulates the automatic processes of the body such as respiration, cardiac activity, coughing and sneezing. It can be further divided into the sympathetic and parasympathetic nervous systems.

> The sympathetic and parasympathetic nervous systems are responsible for opposite functions in the body. If the body is under threat, the sympathetic nervous system kicks into 'fight or flight' mode, preparing the body to fight or flee the threat. The heart rate speeds up and more blood flows through the muscles as they prepare to defend the body. When the body is not under threat, the parasympathetic nervous system regulates resting, digestion and relaxation.

In recent years, research has shown that most people are in 'fight or flight' mode more often than they should be, and are subsequently enduring longer periods of stress. This prolonged stress leads to poorer digestion, poorer quality sleep and an overall degradation of health and wellbeing. It is very important to manage stress and to engage in regular self-care for the health of body and mind.

3   **The enteric nervous system:** This system controls the digestive functions of the body and runs through the central nervous system and the sympathetic nervous system.

The Endocrine System

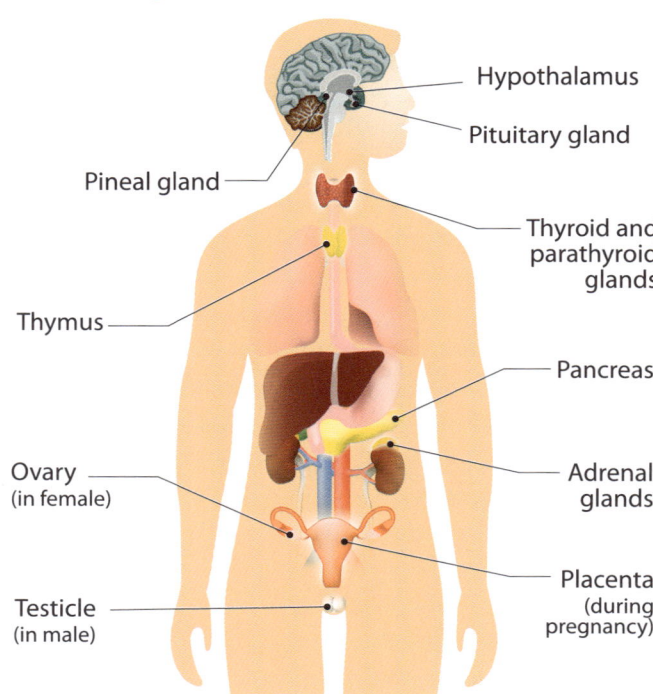

The endocrine system consists of the glands and organs in the body that regulate the making and releasing of hormones for many body processes including growth and development, metabolism, reproduction and responses to events such as stress. The endocrine system is made up of the hypothalamus, the pituitary gland, the pineal gland, the thyroid gland, thymus, adrenal glands, pancreas, ovaries in women and testes in men. We have already looked at the functions of the hypothalamus, pituitary gland and pineal gland. We will now discuss the other glands and organs of the endocrine system.

- **Thyroid gland:** The thyroid gland is located at the base of the neck below the voice box and is butterfly-shaped. It is involved in the metabolism of energy in the body. It also has within it four parathyroid glands that are involved in the amount of calcium present in the body.

- **Thymus:** The thymus is located in the upper chest and is only active up until puberty. It is also part of the lymphatic system (an organ system that is part of the immune system, and complementary to the circulatory system). The thymus produces white blood cells that help fight infection and build up immunity in the body.

- **Adrenal glands:** The adrenal glands are located on top of the kidneys and work with the hypothalamus and pituitary glands. They are responsible for making and releasing hormones involved in controlling blood pressure, metabolism and stress response. In fight or flight mode the adrenal glands play a role in the body defending itself against a threat.

- **Pancreas:** The pancreas is located behind the stomach and across the back of the abdomen. It plays an important part in digestion and is also responsible for hormone production. One of the hormones it secretes is insulin, which controls sugar levels in the blood.

- **Ovaries:** In women, the two ovaries are located on either side of the womb and are where the egg cells for sexual reproduction are stored. Each month during ovulation one egg is secreted. The ovaries also produce different sex hormones including oestrogen and progesterone.

- **Testes:** In men, the testes are located in a sac called the scrotum which hangs outside the body behind the penis. The testes are responsible for making sperm and for the production of the sex hormone testosterone.

Biological Evolution

The evolutionary biologist Charles Darwin (1809–1882) proposed a theory of evolution that outlined how all living things change and develop over time. There were four main parts to his theory:

1. **Competition:** Most species produce more offspring each year than can survive. Therefore, offspring must compete against each other for food and other resources in order to survive.

2. **Inherited traits:** Inherited traits are traits that are passed on from parent to child, for example height or eye colour. If such traits are more likely to improve chances of survival – for example, by being tall enough to reach food on trees – this inherited trait is more likely to be passed on from generation to generation.

3. **Variation:** Every species shows variation or differences in their traits. Even people in the same family have different hair colour, eye colour and height. The environment has an influence on variation, for example in skin tone, hair texture and colour, weight and height.

4. **Survival of the fittest:** Individuals who survive and reproduce pass on to their offspring those traits that helped them survive. As individuals continue to adjust traits to the surrounding

environment, they adapt and become more robust. This is a process known as natural selection (a phrase used by and associated with Darwin but actually coined by fellow biologist Herbert Spencer).

Genetic Psychology

Genetic psychology is a branch of biological psychology that explores the area of genetics in our development. Geneticists are largely focused on the area of deoxyribonucleic acid (DNA) and how the information stored in a person's genes and chromosomes may influence certain illnesses, abnormalities and other behaviour.

Each person has a set of 46 chromosomes in each cell in their body. Each chromosome is made up of two strands of DNA in a double helix. This DNA is passed down from our parents: we receive 23 matching pairs of chromosomes in every cell except for sex cells, which have 23 chromosomes only. During conception, when the egg and sperm fuse, a number of cell divisions take place to form the zygote. These cell divisions are where the genetic material of both parents meet and replicate and the genotype (the genetic constitution) of the person is determined.

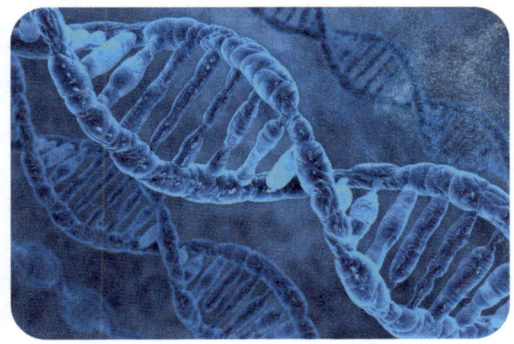

Gregor Mendel and Genes

Czech biologist Gregor Mendel (1822–1884) was one of the pioneers in the field of genetics. He worked with pea plants to investigate how traits are inherited and passed down from generation to generation. By cross-pollinating pea plants he discovered that there were traits that were dominant or that were expressed in the offspring, and other traits that were recessive or that were hidden or masked. His work showed how we can inherit dominant or recessive genes that make up our genotype.

For example, if one parent has brown eyes and the other parent has blue eyes, the child expresses the genotype B for brown eyes and b for blue eyes (Bb) and the phenotype (the observable trait) of brown eyes. (Genotype prediction is represented in a square diagram known as a Punnett square, named after Reginald C. Punnett who devised the approach.)

Harry Harlow and Rhesus Monkeys Experiment

In 1958, American psychologist Harry Harlow conducted a series of what were then and are still considered unethical studies on rhesus monkeys, commonly known as the Pit of Despair experiment. He chose rhesus monkeys because of their genetic similarity to humans. Wanting to ascertain the effect of separation on baby monkeys from their mothers, and thus the effect of similar separation on humans, he gave the infant monkeys a choice between a wire-framed 'mother', which dispensed food, and a cloth-covered 'mother'. Overwhelmingly, the baby monkeys spent most of their time clinging to the cloth mother, only visiting the wire mother for food. Many of these monkeys never recovered from the experiments and developed high anxiety. When they returned to their group they had difficulty forming relationships, and when they went on to have offspring themselves they did not know how to care for them and often mistreated them. John Bowlby and others gained many insights into the nature of attachment from Harlow's findings and went on to do pioneering work in the area of emotional development and child development.

Jane Goodall and the Chimpanzees of Tanzania

English primatologist and anthropologist Jane Goodall spent many years in the Gombe forest of Tanzania studying chimpanzees, becoming the world's foremost expert on them. Her discovery in 1960 that chimpanzees both make and use tools changed the way we view chimpanzees and transformed the relationship that humans have with them and other animals. Goodall's work has given the world many insights into both the behaviour of chimpanzees and the lifetime emotional bonds they create. We now know that chimps and bonobos are our closest living relatives. In 2005, genetic blueprints of humans and chimps showed a DNA sequence match of 96 per cent.

Twin Studies

Twin studies have been used to study the degree of similarity between identical and fraternal twins. Identical twins share 100 per cent genetic information, while fraternal twins share 50 per cent commonality. If similarities can be found in identical twins and those similarities are higher than in fraternal twins, this can be used to prove that genetics play a large role in determining certain behaviour.

Over the years, various studies have been conducted on twins to ascertain how much of a role genetics play in development. Bouchard and McGue (1981) conducted a worldwide study comparing the IQ of family members. Identical twins raised together had the highest correlation at .86, identical twins raised apart scored .72, whereas fraternal twins raised together scored .60. (Flaws were identified, however, in the study's analysis, which would decrease validity.)

Epigenetics

Epigenetics is the study of how the environment and behaviour can cause changes that affect the way genes work. Contrary to the nature-nurture debate, which looks at either genes or environment, epigenetics considers both factors. Epigenetic changes in the body are reversible and do not alter DNA sequence, unlike genetic changes. However, such changes can influence how the body interprets a DNA sequence and this can affect the development and day-to-day operation of a normal cell in the body.

Studies have found that aspects such as exercise, age and diet can influence the way genes work. Each person's epigenetic make-up changes in response to the body's normal growth and development, diet, behaviours and habits. DNA methylation is an essential epigenetic mechanism needed for normal development. As the body ages, DNA methylation levels decrease. Additionally, it has been proven that smokers have reduced levels of DNA methylation. If a person stops smoking, their DNA methylation will increase and over time will return to the levels of a non-smoker.

Studies have also shown that a pregnant woman's diet and nutrition can change the epigenetics of the foetus. One study conducted on adults in the Netherlands who had been in utero during the Dutch famine of 1944–1945 and so subject to lower levels of nutrition showed that as 60-year-olds their methylation levels were increased in some genes and decreased in others in comparison to their siblings gestated earlier or later than this famine period. These 60-year-olds were also more likely to develop diseases such as type 2 diabetes and heart disease.

Therapeutic Interventions in Biological Psychology

Drugs are the primary treatment used in biological psychology. In some cases, treatments such as electroconvulsive therapy (ECT) are used. Here is a list of some drugs used in the treatment of psychological disorders.

Class of drug	Common name	Disorder that it treats
Psychostimulants	Ritalin Adderall	ADHD
Antidepressants	Zoloft Paxil Prozac	Depression and anxiety disorders
Mood stabilisers	Lithobid Depakene	Bipolar disorder
Anti-anxiety drugs	Xanax Valium	Panic, anxiety and mood disorders
Antipsychotic drugs	Zyprexa Haldol Thorazine	Schizophrenia

Criticisms of Biological Psychology

Biological psychology has been criticised from the point of view of not addressing nurture and focusing primarily on nature or genetics. As well as that, drug therapy can have side effects and needs to be monitored closely, while brain therapies such as ECT need to be executed with extreme care and caution.

> **Review what you have learned**
>
> 1. Name the two parts that make up the human nervous system.
> 2. Identify one important neurotransmitter, its function, and its sources.
> 3. Name the largest part of the brain and list what it is responsible for.
> 4. Name the four lobes of the brain.
> 5. Identify the three systems of the peripheral nervous system.
> 6. Write a short description of the pancreas.
> 7. Define the terms 'genotype' and 'phenotype'.
> 8. Define 'epigenetics'.
> 9. Name one drug used to treat depression.

Here is a recap of what has been covered to date.

Perspective	Founders	Principles	Therapies	Limitations
Psycho-analysis	Sigmund Freud Anna Freud Carl Rogers Erik Erikson John Bowlby	The unconscious mind The id, the ego and the superego Archetypes and personality	Free association Dream analysis Transference Play therapy and art therapy	Lacking scientific basis/quantitative data Theories critiqued as 'overly simple' Over-emphasis on sex and childhood development
Behaviourism	Ivan Pavlov John B. Watson B.F. Skinner	Classical conditioning Operant conditioning	Aversive conditioning Exposure therapy Systematic desensitisation	Many experiments conducted on animals, therefore not readily applicable to humans Different genetic or biological dispositions not taken into account, with over-emphasis on environment as determining behaviour

(Cont. overleaf)

Perspective	Founders	Principles	Therapies	Limitations
Humanistic Psychology	Abraham Maslow Carl Rogers	Maslow's Hierarchy of Needs Self-actualisation	Person-centred therapy Transpersonal therapy Play therapy Mindfulness	Subjective Unquantifiable
Cognitive Psychology	Jean Piaget Albert Ellis Aaron Beck Lev Vygotsky	Piaget's stages of cognitive development ABC model Cognitive triad Cognitive dissonance	REBT CBT	Cannot be directly observed (i.e. cannot see what is going on inside the brain) Does not take other factors into account
Biological Psychology	Charles Darwin Gregor Mendel Harry Harlow Jane Goodall	The nervous system Neurotransmitters Hormones The endocrine system Evolution Genetics and epigenetics Twin studies	Drug therapy ECT	Does not take other factors (e.g. environment) into account Drug and ECT therapies are high risk

chapter 8
BRANCHES OF PSYCHOLOGY – DEVELOPMENTAL PSYCHOLOGY

IN THIS CHAPTER YOU WILL LEARN ABOUT:

- developmental psychology
- Mary Ainsworth and attachment styles
- Diana Baumrind and parenting styles
- Urie Bronfenbrenner and ecological systems
- lifespan development
- therapeutic interventions in developmental psychology
- criticisms of developmental psychology.

What is Developmental Psychology?

Developmental psychology is the scientific study of how and why human beings change over the course of their life. It seeks to examine and explain growth and development throughout the human life cycle, using different frameworks to understand how and why people develop, change and adapt. Developmental psychologists include Erik Erikson (Chapter 3), Jean Piaget (Chapter 6), Mary Ainsworth, Diana Baumrind and Urie Bronfenbrenner.

Mary Ainsworth and Attachment Styles

A student of John Bowlby, American-Canadian developmental psychologist Mary Ainsworth progressed Bowlby's work and developed experiments to find out more about attachment styles, the most notable and best known of which was the 'Strange Situation Classification'. This experiment was based around infants aged 12 to 18 months and attempted to explore the interactions between them, their mother and a stranger to ascertain whether or not the infant would exhibit separation anxiety when not in the presence of the mother/when in the presence of a stranger.

Focus on ... Mary Ainsworth (1913–1999)

Mary Ainsworth was born in Glendale, Ohio in 1913, the eldest of three girls. Both of her parents were college graduates and encouraged Mary to get a college education. Ainsworth earned a doctorate degree in psychology from the University of Toronto and began teaching at that university in 1938. Moving to London in 1950 to pursue further study, she met and worked with John Bowlby. They researched the effects of interference on the mother and child bond. She went on to develop the 'Strange Situation' with Sylvia Bell. This method of measuring attachment in children is still in use today.

Strange Situation Procedure

- The mother and child are brought into a room and allowed to settle for one minute.
- The mother and child play together with toys for three minutes.
- The stranger enters the room and sits down quietly for one minute, chats to the mother for one minute and then plays with the child for one minute.

- The mother then says goodbye to the child and leaves the room for three minutes.
- The mother then returns and the stranger leaves. The mother offers herself as a comfort to the child (e.g. by holding out her arms) if the child seeks comforting.
- The mother leaves again and the child is left alone for three minutes.
- The stranger returns and comforts the child if the child seeks comforting.
- After three minutes, the mother returns and the stranger leaves. Again the mother offers herself as a comfort to the child if the child seeks comforting.

Ainsworth and her researchers analysed the reunion phase and, looking for certain behaviours, observed and scored infants. From their findings they identified four distinctive attachment styles.

1. **Secure attachment:** Sixty-five to 70 per cent of infants were in this category. These infants were more likely to cry when the mother left the room and were less likely to be calmed down by the stranger. They were calmed down by their mother when she returned and appeared to be happy and trusting of the comfort their mother gave them. When they were calm they were able to return to play with the toys once again.

2. **Insecure-avoidant attachment:** Ten to 15 per cent of infants were in this category. These children were not as likely to be upset when their mother left the room and when she re-entered the room did not usually look for her to comfort them. They were more receptive to the stranger than securely attached children, even when alone with the stranger.

3. **Insecure-resistant attachment:** Fifteen to 20 per cent of infants were in this category. They cried a lot when the mother

left the room. However, when the mother re-entered the room, they were resistant and did not always seek comfort from her. Even if they did seek comfort they were not always reassured by the mother and often continued to be upset for longer than securely attached children.

4. **Disorganised attachment:** About five per cent of infants were in this category. Some were upset when the mother left the room and some were not. When the mother re-entered the room they were not sure exactly what to do and exhibited mixed responses to the mother, either resisting and then avoiding or avoiding and then resisting. In follow-ups, this group of children seemed to fare the worst in life.

Diana Baumrind and Parenting Styles

Diana Baumrind was an American developmental psychologist who studied the behaviour of preschool children. She believed there to be a correlation between parent behaviour and child behaviour and conducted observations and interviews as part of her research. According to Baumrind, different parenting styles lead to different types of children with different development patterns and outcomes for their lives. The three different types of parenting she identified were as follows:

1. **Authoritative:** This parenting style gives a child a high level of boundaries but also a high level of choice, interaction, support and praise. This parent will offer more choice and freedom within reason and will also listen to and validate the child in their day-to-day interactions. They will continually explain and communicate with the child about their expectations of them. They will also give clear consequences and rules for unacceptable behaviour. The consequence of this parenting style is a child who is more independent, has high self-esteem, displays better interaction with peers and is happy and capable.

BRANCHES OF PSYCHOLOGY – DEVELOPMENTAL PSYCHOLOGY

2. **Authoritarian:** This parenting style gives a child a high level of boundaries and rules but not much input on choices or decision-making. The parent establishes the behaviour a child must exhibit and choices a child must make and rewards accordingly. If the child does not do what the parent requests, there are consequences such as negative reinforcement and punishment. If the child behaves as desired by the parent, they will be praised and given other positive reinforcements. The consequence of this parenting style is a child who follows rules and authority and who scores lower on self-esteem, social skills and happiness than a child of authoritative parents.

3. **Permissive:** Also known as indulgent parenting, this style gives a child a low level of boundaries but a high level of support, choice and freedom. The child has very little consequences for inappropriate behaviour and gets minimum direction from the parent. The consequence of this parenting style is a child who usually has more problems with authority and who scores lower on self-esteem, social skills and happiness than a child of authoritative or authoritarian parents.

Later, Maccoby and Martin (1992) would add a fourth parenting style:

4. **Uninvolved/Neglectful:** This parenting style gives a child a low level of boundaries and support. This child ranks lower than all other children on self-esteem, happiness, self-control and peer interaction.

Parenting Style	Boundaries/Rules	Support/Interaction/Praise
Authoritative	high	high
Authoritarian	high	low
Permissive	low	high
Uninvolved	low	low

> ### Focus on ... Diana Baumrind (1927–2018)
>
> Diana Baumrind was born in 1927 in New York, USA. She grew up in the Jewish community and had one sister. Receiving a BA in Psychology and Philosophy in 1948 from Hunter College, she went on to complete a PhD at the University of California in Berkeley. Baumrind was a developmental and clinical psychologist at the Institute of Human Development, University of California, where she researched parenting styles and the effects of corporal punishment on children.

Apply your learning

> Using the three case studies from page 34, state what each parenting style means for the development of each of the children using what you have learned from Baumrind's work.

Case study 1: Aoife

Aoife is eight months and is in stage 1 of Erikson's theory. Aoife is being raised by her father and he is bottle feeding.

Aoife's father is authoritative in his parenting style. What does this mean for Aoife and her development?

Case study 2: Maeve

Maeve is two years six months and is in stage 2 of Erikson's theory. She is wetting the bed most nights and is getting very upset by this.

Maeve's caregivers are authoritarian in their parenting style. What does this mean for Maeve and her development?

Case study 3: Joe

Joe is four and is in stage 3 of Erikson's theory. Joe is adapting to a change in family structure following the arrival of his baby sister.

Joe's parents are permissive in their parenting style. What does this mean for Joe and his development?

Urie Bronfenbrenner and Ecological Systems

Urie Bronfenbrenner was a Russian developmental psychologist who developed the ecological systems theory. Bronfenbrenner examined the environment of the child and identified four different systems that influenced their life and development.

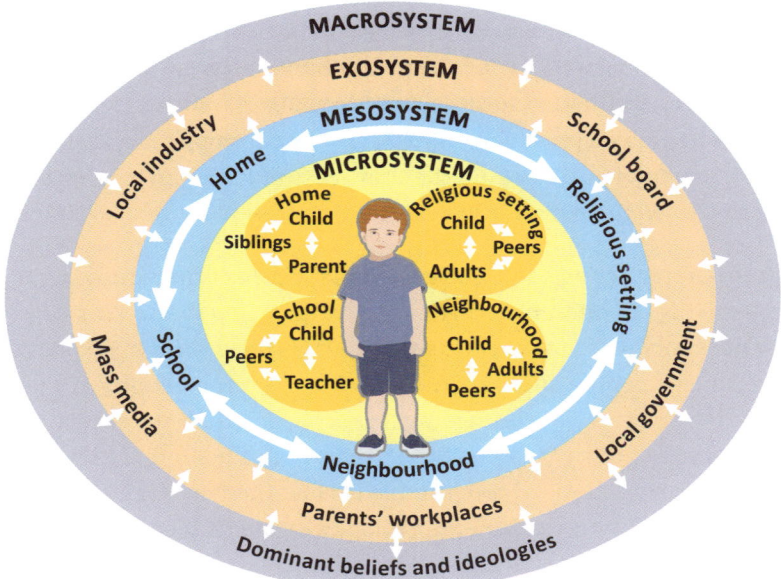

1 **Microsystem:** This is the system that has the most direct influence on a child in their daily life and includes the child's family, peers, childcare environment, school environment, neighbours, etc.

2 **Mesosystem:** These are the relationships between the microsystems, for example a parent attending a parent–teacher meeting, or two parents in the neighbourhood planning a party, etc.

3 **Exosystem:** These are factors that are not directly in the child's environment but which have an effect on the child nonetheless. Examples include a parent's working conditions, access to health insurance, the available resources in the larger community, etc.

4. **Macrosystem:** This is the larger cultural context in which the child lives and includes the attitudes and beliefs in that culture about aspects such as religion, education and societal values.

Focus on ... Urie Bronfenbrenner (1917–2005)

Urie Bronfenbrenner was born in Moscow in 1917. His family immigrated to the USA when Urie was six to escape the Russian revolution. Earning a scholarship to Cornell University in 1934, where he studied psychology, Bronfenbrenner completed a PhD in developmental psychology at the University of Michigan before going on to Cornell University to work as a developmental psychologist.

Bronfenbrenner was very interested in the role of the family in the raising of children. He believed that following World War II, by necessity more parents worked full-time to pay bills and keep the house running and were thus leaving the responsibility of childrearing to other settings such as schools. Bronfenbrenner helped to establish the Head Start Program in 1965, a federally funded early childhood programme for low-income families. He is best known for his work on the ecological systems theory.

Apply your learning

Examine again the case of Joe and complete an ecological system for him.

Case study 3: Joe

Joe is four and is in stage 3 of Erikson's theory. Joe is adapting to a change in family structure following the arrival of his baby sister. Joe's parents are permissive in their parenting style.

BRANCHES OF PSYCHOLOGY – DEVELOPMENTAL PSYCHOLOGY

> Joe lives in a busy residential area in Dublin and has just started primary school. His two close friends from preschool live on the same road as him, and there is also a local park and community centre close by which he often visits for activity and sport. His father works in the building trade and his mother works in the local credit union. They are now converting Joe's playroom downstairs into a bedroom for his granny, Ann, as she is going to live with them following the death of Joe's granddad, Jim.
>
> Describe Joe's ecological system and the factors influencing his life and development.

Lifespan Development

Lifespan development explores the changes experienced throughout life. Freud and Erikson both proposed lifespan development theories, focusing on the changes that a human goes through as they grow, change and develop. In general terms, the lifespan of a human being can be broken down into different phases and this is based on normative development, or the average time it takes to develop in these different phases, which gives us general guidelines for human behaviour and overall development.

Prenatal development: This is the phase concerning conception (the fusing of egg and sperm). It follows the development from the germinal, embryonic and foetal stages and explores the changes from zygote to foetus. Developmental psychologists are interested in foetal development and responses exhibited by the foetus to negative stressors such as alcohol, drugs and smoking (teratogens). Also

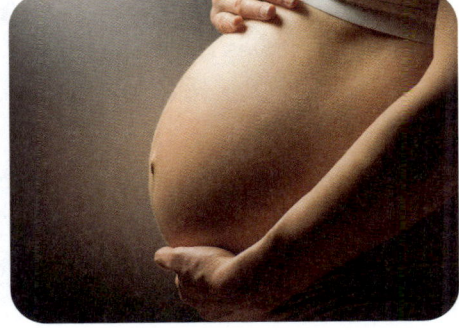

researched are the development of the brain and organs and other effects arising out of the choices of the mother in relation to diet, nutrition and lifestyle, as well as external social and emotional concerns.

Infancy: This is the phase from birth to one year. In this stage the infant is rapidly growing, exploring and developing. Most primary reflexes resolve in this period of development and on average most infants begin to walk around one year. Developmental psychologists are interested in the rapid changes exhibited by infants, who are exploring the world, absorbing large amounts of information and developing the ability to recognise things and people and to recall information.

Toddler: This is the phase from ages one to three. Again there is a huge amount of growth and brain development in this stage. The child is becoming more autonomous, learning how to use the potty, feed and dress themselves. This is another critical period of early childhood. Developmental psychologists are interested in the continued rapid changes being exhibited. The child will go through many normative milestones, including developing more refined fine and gross motor skills and more complex language and communication. If during this stage a child is not meeting their normative milestones, a developmental psychologist may be asked to examine the

issue further. Research has shown that early intervention is very positive when it comes to helping a child with a delay. However it should be noted that all children are unique and that not meeting certain milestones at this stage does not necessarily indicate a clinical issue.

Preschool: This is the phase from ages three to five and is considered the last stage in early childhood. At this stage and depending on the culture, most children will spend some time in a crèche or with a childminder. The child is refining both fine and gross motor skills, developing emotional and social skills and forming friendships. Developmental psychologists are interested in the continued normative development of the child in this stage.

School-age child: This is the phase from ages six to 12. At this stage the child is in the primary school setting and the focus is on school life, schoolwork and peer relationships. The child strives to do well at school and to develop friendships with classmates, locally or in sports or clubs. If there are any social, emotional or mental health issues in this stage, a parent or school may consult with a developmental psychologist.

Adolescence: This is the phase from ages 13 to 19. This is the time of puberty and hormonal changes. At this stage the adolescent is focused on peer relationships and on their identity in the group. They explore their identity and gain interest in intimacy and sexual relationships. They strive to make sense of the world and their place in it. The prefrontal cortex, located in the frontal lobe, is still developing, and adolescents may engage in more experimentation and risk-taking behaviour. Developmental psychologists are particularly interested in the changes wrought by the internal biological changes being visited on the body at this stage.

> According to David Elkind (1967), adolescence has four characteristics:
>
> 1 Adolescent egocentrism – An adolescent believes that their time and needs are more important than anybody else's.
>
> 2 Imaginary audience – An adolescent believes that others are focusing all their attention on them.
>
> 3 Personal fable – An adolescent believes that nobody else could ever understand them because they are truly unique. They do not think that anyone else has ever gone through the same situation as them.
>
> 4 Vulnerability illusion – An adolescent believes that bad things will only happen to other people and never to them.

Adulthood: This is the phase from ages 20 to end of life. It can be broken down into early, middle and late adulthood. New brain research has now found that the adult brain is not fully developed until age 25 so technically it could be argued that adulthood begins at this age. This is the last stage of human development before death, where adults usually find a partner, have children or create a family and start and develop a career before entering retirement. Some issues explored by developmental psychologists at this stage are mental health, career, family life and work/life balance.

Task
Think-Pair-Share
Complete a chart, poster or graphic of a list of milestones for each lifespan phase, then pair and share what you came up with.

Therapeutic Interventions in Developmental Psychology

Developmental psychologists might work in schools, hospitals or assisted living facilities. In the instance of a parent or school being concerned about the progress of a child or young person, a developmental psychologist will administer a screening test. An educational psychologist or child psychologist may also be involved in administering and evaluating various types of tests. An educational psychologist will examine intelligence tests while a child psychologist will conduct observations to ascertain whether or not a child is meeting normative milestones. The child will then be referred to other services as deemed necessary, such as speech therapy, physical therapy or occupational therapy.

A developmental psychologist can help someone at any stage of their life if they are struggling with developmental issues. Older people may be assisted by developmental psychologists in relation to various daily tasks and routine.

Criticisms of Developmental Psychology

Stage theories and normative milestones are used by developmental psychologists to assess what is expected of the average individual. However, these theories can be too rigid and often fail to capture the full picture of what is going on. Not all children or people adhere to normative patterns or theories, and there may not be any cause for concern should they not. Further holistic exploration is often needed when assessing an individual.

Many stage theories were developed using children and much of the work from developmental psychology has been conducted on children. Children present their own issues during research including attention span, comprehension and consent.

Review what you have learned

1. In your own words, explain the aim of developmental psychology.
2. Explain in brief Mary Ainsworth's 'Strange Situation' experiment and list the attachment styles it gave rise to.
3. Name and explain the three parenting styles, according to Baumrind.
4. Give an outline of Bronfenbrenner's ecological systems theory.
5. In your own words, explain what lifespan development is.

chapter 9

BRANCHES OF PSYCHOLOGY – ABNORMAL PSYCHOLOGY

IN THIS CHAPTER YOU WILL LEARN ABOUT:

- abnormal psychology
- how abnormal behaviour is determined
- how abnormal behaviour is diagnosed
- types of abnormal disorders
- therapeutic interventions in abnormal psychology
- criticisms of abnormal psychology.

What is Abnormal Psychology?

Abnormal psychology, often referred to as clinical psychology or psycho-pathology, is a branch of psychology that deals with psychological disorders. These types of disorders are usually called mental disorders or mental illness.

A recent study conducted by the Organisation for Economic Co-operation and Development showed that Ireland has one of the highest rates of mental health issues in Europe, with 18.5 per cent of the population reporting a mental health illness. A 2018 survey regarding mental health and recovery carried out by Mental Health Ireland showed that women reported lower wellbeing scores than men, young people lower scores than older people and unemployed people and full-time homemakers lower scores than those working full- or part-time. However, 93 per cent of participants were aware of things they could do to improve their mental health and wellbeing, citing exercise, talking to someone, healthy eating, counselling, meditation and yoga. Awareness around mental health has certainly grown in recent years, with more people now willing to discuss it, despite ongoing stigma around the topic, and with a growing range of tools and apps designed to help people deal with daily life and its stressors.

Determining Abnormal Behaviour

Everyone copes differently with situations that could be deemed stressful, so how do we ascertain what is 'normal' behaviour and what is 'abnormal' behaviour? Though it is difficult to provide a straightforward definition of abnormality because of its subjective nature, psychologists often classify abnormal behaviour according to the 'four Ds': the **dysfunction** it creates for the individual; the **distress** caused to the individual and those around them; the nature of their behaviour which, according to cultural and societal norms, could be classified as **deviant**; and whether or not the behaviour is **dangerous**.

Dysfunction

Dysfunction is defined as not being able to carry out daily tasks or activities because of a breakdown in cognitive, emotional or social behaviour. If a person cannot function due to a dysfunctional behaviour, this is described as being abnormal.

For example: A person spending a lot of time cleaning and organising, as well as washing their hands and sanitising everything around them, may not be able to leave the house until their cleaning rituals have been completed and may not be able to interact with other people or places for fear of germs or lack of cleanliness. This behaviour would impact on the person's relationships, time, interactions and overall wellbeing. It would also impact the other people living or closely associating with this person.

Distress

If the behaviours of an individual lead to moderate to extreme distress and this distress interferes with the person's ability to function in daily life and activities, then this type of ongoing distress is defined as abnormal. It is normal that a person will become distressed in life from time to time and this is not seen as a problem. However, if a person's behaviour frequently causes them and others around them stress and distress, this would need further investigation.

For example: A person who fears social interactions may not want to engage in social events and activities or relationships and may not be able to work. If a person minimises interactions and cannot function in work or engage in friendships and intimate relationships, this would greatly impact on their quality of life and of those around them.

Deviancy

Deviant behaviour is anything that is deemed unacceptable in a particular society. Different cultures have different norms or expectations for people in that society. If someone acts against those norms and does not actively 'fit in', this is viewed as abnormal. This is a tricky area, however, as different cultures have different social norms and customs; what is viewed as 'abnormal' in one culture may not be viewed as such in another. Cultural norms also change as societies change.

For example: In the recent past in Ireland it was considered deviant to be homosexual. Now in this country attitudes towards the LGBT+ community are among the most liberal in the world. However, in other countries throughout the world homosexuality is still considered a deviancy and there are societal and cultural 'norms' in place to uphold this attitude. Behaviour classified as deviant in Ireland today would include excessive alcohol consumption, drink-driving or drug use.

Danger

A person having thoughts, feelings or emotions that make them want to harm themselves or others is said to be exhibiting abnormal behaviour. Anger is a natural emotion, and we often need to release 'negative' energy, but we learn as young children how to regulate and control our emotions in a healthy way. If a person has behaviours that are destructive and are dangerous to themselves or others, this needs to be investigated further.

For example: Self-harming as a result of thoughts, feelings or emotions is a behaviour that causes harm and ultimately distress to both the individual and to those around them.

It is important to note that fulfilling one of these criteria does not necessarily mean that someone is suffering from a mental disorder. In many cases, abnormal behaviour patterns have to be explored and much more detail gathered about a person and their own unique situation before any diagnosis can be given. Extreme care must be taken and correct protocol followed when it comes to diagnosis.

BRANCHES OF PSYCHOLOGY – ABNORMAL PSYCHOLOGY

Task

Think-Pair-Share
Can you think of other examples of the four Ds in abnormal behaviour? Fill in the table, then pair and share what you came up with.

Abnormal Criteria	Example
Dysfunction	
Deviancy	
Distress	
Danger	

Diagnosing Abnormal Behaviour

DSM-V

The *Diagnostic and Statistical Manual* (DSM) is a handbook used mainly in the USA for the diagnosis of mental health disorders. There have been several versions or revisions to the DSM since it was first published in 1952 (DSM-I), with the current edition having been published in 2013 (DSM-V). The handbook contains symptoms, descriptions and other criteria for diagnosing a person with a disorder. It also gives other information such as typical age of onset of the disorder, treatments for the disorder, gender most affected by the disorder, and so on. To attain treatment, the government requires that a person has a diagnosis, and insurance companies also require proof of diagnosis to provide cover for treatment.

ICD 11

The *International Classification of Diseases 11th Revision* (ICD 11) is a global categorisation system regarding physical and mental health disorders developed and updated by the World Health Organization. Development of this edition started in 2007, spanning over a decade of work and containing about 85,000 entities (an entity can be anything relevant to healthcare). Available electronically, it has been translated into 43 different languages for worldwide accessibility. Additions to this version include attention deficit disorder, gaming disorder and complex post-traumatic disorder.

Abnormal Disorders

DSM-V lists categories of mental disorders along with some related disorders. There are currently 157 disorders listed in this DSM. Examples of categories include the following:

- **Anxiety disorders:** This category includes phobias, generalised anxiety disorder, panic disorders and trauma disorders.
- **Autism spectrum disorder:** This includes anyone on the autism spectrum; Asperger's is now included in this category.
- **Bipolar and related mood disorders:** This includes substance-induced mood disorder and health-related mood disorder.
- **Depressive disorders:** This includes major depressive disorder, postpartum depression, seasonal affective disorder and premenstrual dysphoric disorder.
- **Feeding and other related disorders:** This includes binge-eating disorders, anorexia nervosa, bulimia nervosa and other food-related disorders.
- **Obsessive compulsive and related disorders:** This includes OCD disorder, hoarding disorder and body dysmorphic disorder.

- **Personality disorders:** This includes paranoid personality disorder, antisocial personality disorder, borderline personality disorder, narcissistic personality disorder, avoidant personality disorder and dependent personality disorder.

- **Schizophrenia and other psychotic disorders:** This includes brief psychotic disorder, delusional disorder and schizoaffective disorder.

> **Task**
>
> **Think-Pair-Share**
> Think about the advantages and disadvantages of using DSM-V to obtain a diagnosis. An example of each is given here. Pair and share your thoughts.
>
> | Advantage | Disadvantage |
> |---|---|
> | Insurance will pay for treatment with a diagnosis | A diagnosis may be over-simplified |
> | | |
> | | |
> | | |

Therapeutic Interventions in Abnormal Psychology

There are various different treatments for mental disorders depending on the perspective taken by the psychologist dealing with the case. Often it is effective to use a few modalities in the treatment plan; for example, a person may take medication for a time as well as receiving therapy.

- Various techniques such as cognitive behavioural therapy, rational emotive behavioural therapy and exposure therapy are used by qualified therapists.

- Alternative therapies may be also used by a person to manage the disorder including acupuncture, aromatherapy, Chinese medicine, naturopathy, homoeopathy and mindfulness techniques.

- Medication is sometimes used, with different types of drugs available for different disorders. Medication can only be prescribed to a patient by a GP or psychiatrist. (See Chapter 7, page 87 for a list of drugs and the conditions they are used to treat.)

- Electroconvulsive therapy (ECT) is the application of a brief electric stimulus to the brain to create a seizure. In use since the 1940s in the US to treat people with severe mental health issues, it is still used today worldwide in the treatment of people with certain mood disorders, most commonly severe depression.

Criticisms of Abnormal Psychology

The field of abnormal psychology has been accused of stigmatising vulnerable and oppressed people and people who exhibit behaviours outside of the cultural norm. The argument is also made that abnormal psychology tends to pathologise normal variations in human behaviour. As well as that, there is always the risk that a diagnosis will be made in error. And while a correct diagnosis (or what is deemed correct by the field) can be beneficial to the individual in some regards, there is still the strong risk that it will negatively label and brand the individual.

Review what you have learned

1. List the four Ds in abnormal behaviour.
2. Explain in your own words one category of abnormal disorder as listed in DSM-V.
3. What is ECT and when is it used?

chapter 10
RESEARCH METHODS IN PSYCHOLOGY

IN THIS CHAPTER YOU WILL LEARN ABOUT:

- the scientific method in psychology
- types of research design in psychology
- checking the reliability of sources.

Scientific Method in Psychology

In order to reach measurable conclusions in relation to human thought and behaviour, some schools of psychology apply a scientific method:

1. Ask a question
2. Carry out research
3. Form a hypothesis
4. Conduct experiments
5. Collect data
6. Analyse data
7. Draw conclusions, which prove, partially prove or do not prove hypothesis
8. Communicate results

9 Carry out further research or return to original question and reframe.

This process not only allows scientists to investigate and understand different psychological phenomena, but also provides researchers and others with a way to share and discuss the results of their studies.

For example, consider the question 'Do children who are breastfed have a higher IQ than children who are not breastfed?' The psychologist would first investigate research already carried out in this area. Next, a hypothesis about children who have been breastfed will be created (e.g. 'Children who are breastfed have a higher IQ than those who are not') and the psychologist will try to design a study and conduct experiments that will show it to be right or wrong. Data is then collected and analysed and conclusions drawn regarding the hypothesis and whether or not it can be proved.

There are many different kinds of studies, but all have common problems such as trying to isolate the behaviour that is to be studied (in this case, IQ level; for example, how can the researcher be sure that breastfeeding is the only reason that someone has a higher IQ than someone who is not breastfed?) Such 'confounding factors' (a third variable in a study examining cause-and-effect relationships) can explain the results of an experiment but remain outside the scope of measurable factors as determined by the experiment.

Qualitative and Quantitate Data

In order to prove or disprove a hypothesis, information or data must be collected. The type of data that is to be gathered has to be considered before the research method is decided upon. Data can be either qualitative or quantitative. Qualitative data deals with words and meanings while quantitative data deals with numbers and statistics. Qualitative data is usually based on personal opinion and experiences and is usually harder to capture numerically, e.g. testimonials, interviews, case studies and photos. Quantitative data is based on facts and figures and is usually easier to measure, e.g. responses on a survey, age, height, weight and IQ.

Primary and Secondary Research Sources

Data can come from primary or secondary sources. Primary sources are sources that come directly from the source. Examples include eyewitness testimonies, written accounts (e.g. a diary), photographs, recorded interviews or artefacts. Secondary sources are sources that do not come directly from the source but are closely related to them, often interpreting them. Examples include evaluation and analysis of primary sources in books, articles or journals.

Types of Research Design in Psychology

There are a number of different types of research design used in psychology, including descriptive, correlational, experimental, diagnostic and explanatory. Here we will look at the first three.

Descriptive Research Design

Descriptive studies aim to gather data to present a picture of a given subject or issue. Descriptive designs include surveys, case studies and naturalistic observation (see table below).

Educational psychologists might use a survey to assess the IT level of students in a secondary school. The results would not tell them anything about the IT level of the students' families, but it would give a complete picture of the students' IT levels in the school environment.

Psychologists might use a case study if they want to get a complete picture of one person in particular. Case studies examine an individual closely in order to find out about them and gain an insight into their behaviour and motivations.

Naturalistic observations are observations that take place in the subject's natural environment. Jean Piaget carried out many naturalistic observations of his own and his friends' children in their homes. This is the least intrusive type of descriptive design that can be used in psychological research.

Descriptive design can lead to correlational design and experimental design.

Descriptive Research Design Types	Data	Source	Uses in Psychology
Survey	Quantitative	Primary	Used to gather large or small amounts of data about specific information; for example, the census is a survey that captures many details about the population including age, marital status and number of children
Case study	Qualitative or quantitative	Primary or secondary	Used to explore one particular subject or topic in depth as detail and specific information can be obtained
Observation	Qualitative or quantitative	Primary	Used to observe specific patterns or behaviour, tracking progression over time; used particularly in child development to chart progression in different domains of development
Experiment	Quantitative	Primary	Used to test a hypothesis in order to see if it is valid; usually conducted in a controlled lab environment

Descriptive Research Design Types	Data	Source	Uses in Psychology
Interview	Qualitative	Primary	Used to gather first-hand information and details from a person
Literature review	Qualitative or quantitative	Secondary	Used to take a second-hand look at an area or topic in order to gain new information or ask further questions on that topic

Correlational Research Design

Correlational studies look at the relationship between two or more variables. A variable is anything that is liable to change and that can be measured, for example age. In correlational studies, two groups may be compared; for example, children who were breastfed and children who were not breastfed may be tested for intelligence levels. A correlation is represented by a number called the Pearson correlation coefficient. This number ranges from −1 to 1. If two variables have a correlation of 0, it means that there is no relationship between them. For example, date of birth and eye colour have no correlation, therefore they are said to have a correlation of 0. A correlation between 0 and 1 is deemed 'positive', and it means that as the first variable increases, so does the second one. This turns out to be true in the case of breastfed children and intelligence: breastfed children at age eight had an overall higher IQ score than children who were not breastfed (*BMC Pregnancy and Childbirth*, 21(62) [2021]).

An important shortcoming of correlational research is the problem of determining causation (the action of causing something). Correlation is not causation. Though there is a mild positive correlation between breastfeeding and children's IQ, this does not mean that breastfeeding is the only thing that causes a child's high IQ. It is possible that high IQs are caused by other factors such as parents' IQ level, income level and socioeconomic status.

Experimental Research Design

In experimental research psychologists try to control all the variables in tightly controlled laboratory conditions. Experimental psychology attempts to gather information about human thoughts, feelings and behaviour. Wilhelm Wundt opened the first experimental psychology laboratory in Leipzig, Germany in the late 1800s. He was influenced by the work of German experimental psychologist Gustav Fechner, who researched human perception in the 1830s and was one of the first scientists to work on psychological experimentation and human mental states. Wundt developed and made concrete what Fechner had set out in his early work.

Experimental psychology always has both independent and dependent variables. An independent variable is something that the psychologist changes. The dependent variable is the variable or variables that change depending on the independent variable. In the case of the Little Albert experiment (p. 42), the noise to which Albert was exposed was the independent variable manipulated by Watson, and the dependent variable was the fear that Albert displayed when the white rat was paired with the loud noise.

A confounding variable is a variable that could have an effect on the independent or dependent variables and therefore is something that a psychologist tries to prevent from entering an experiment.

> **Task** **Think-Pair-Share**
> Can you think of any confounding variables in the case of baby Albert? Pair and share your thoughts.

In some experiments two groups may be set up: an experimental group and a control group. In this instance the experimental group may undergo a treatment or manipulation of an independent variable, while the control group will not undergo any treatment or manipulation of the independent variable. Subsequently, both groups will be measured for results to see if there were any changes in the experimental group.

Checking Validity and Reliability of Sources

Checking the validity and reliability of sources throughout research is very important. For example, considering literature, does the author have any vested interest in the topic that would therefore make them skew results or opinions? Does the author include citations for the article so that the information can be cross-checked? Has the text been checked or peer reviewed by other experts in the area, therefore supporting its validity?

To check if a literature source is reliable the following must be considered:

- Date of source: Is the source current? How long ago was it published?

- Author: Who is the author? Are they an expert in the area? Might they have any personal gain in writing the article/book/news story? Is the author linked to any reputable organisation?

- Publisher: Who is the publisher? Where are they based? Are they reputable/linked to reputable organisations?

- Research method: What research method was used to gather data? Is it relevant?

Regarding checking the validity of other types of primary sources:

- **Eyewitness accounts:** If you are using a direct eyewitness account, it needs to be ascertained that the person really did witness the event.
- **Interviews:** If you are interviewing someone, you must check that they fit the criteria of your research before you interview them.
- **Gathering data:** If you are gathering data via a survey, make sure that your questions are not biased in favour of a desired outcome.

> **Review what you have learned**
>
> 1. List the steps in the scientific method for designing a study in psychology.
> 2. What is qualitative data? How can it be gathered?
> 3. What is quantitative data? How can it be gathered?
> 4. Give two examples of primary source material.
> 5. Give one example of secondary source material.
> 6. Identify and explain one type of research design in psychology.

chapter 11
ETHICAL ISSUES IN PSYCHOLOGY AND RESEARCH

IN THIS CHAPTER YOU WILL LEARN ABOUT:

- ethics in psychology
- ethical considerations in research
- examples of unethical psychological experiments.

Ethics in Psychology

Ethics is a system that governs our code of conduct and determines what is right and wrong in terms of our actions. The Psychological Society of Ireland (PSI) is the professional psychological body in Ireland. Founded in 1970 and representing approximately 4,000 members, it is 'committed to maintaining the high standards of practice in psychology'. Its aims and activities include the following:

- Advance and promote the discipline of psychology
- Promote high standards of training and education for psychologists in Ireland
- Promote high professional and ethical standards within the profession

- Provide professional learning, development and networking opportunities
- Sustain growth in PSI membership
- Annual scientific and professional conferences
- Public talks and media communications
- Update members on psychology matters in Ireland.

(https://www.psychologicalsociety.ie/about)

The PSI Code of Professional Ethics consists of four overall ethical principles, which subsume a large number of specific ethical standards.

Principle 1 Respect for the rights and dignity of the person

This principle requires of psychologists that they treat their clients as persons of intrinsic worth with a right to determine their own priorities, that they respect clients' dignity, and give due regard to their moral and cultural values. Psychologists shall take care not to intrude inappropriately on clients' privacy. They shall treat as confidential all information (including oral, verbal, written and electronic) obtained in the course of their work, except where the law requires disclosure. As far as possible, they shall ensure that clients understand and consent to whatever professional action they propose.

Principle 2 Competence

Psychologists must constantly maintain and update their professional skills and ethical awareness. They shall recognise that psychological knowledge and their own expertise and capacity for work are limited, and take care not to exceed the limits.

Principle 3 Responsibility

In their professional and scientific activities, psychologists are required to act in a trustworthy, reputable and accountable manner towards clients and the community. They shall avoid doing harm to clients and research participants, and act to prevent harm caused by others. They shall cooperate with colleagues and other professionals to ensure the best service to clients, and act positively to resolve ethical dilemmas. They shall ensure that those whom they supervise act ethically. In research with animals, they shall take care to treat the animals humanely.

Principle 4 Integrity

Psychologists are obliged to be honest and accurate about their qualifications, the effectiveness of the services which they offer and their research findings. They shall take steps to manage personal stress and maintain their own mental health. They shall treat others in a fair, open and straightforward manner, honour professional commitments and act to clarify any confusion about their role or responsibilities. Where possible, they shall avoid the use of deception with research participants. They shall not use the professional relationship to exploit clients, sexually or otherwise, and they shall deal actively with conflicts of interest. They shall take action against harmful or unethical behaviour in colleagues or members of other professions.

(https://www.psychologicalsociety.ie/Article/Code-of-Ethics-1)

Ethical Considerations in Research

Why do ethics in research matter? Over the course of history there have been many experimental research studies that were unethical. They did not protect human rights, human dignity and respect. Oftentimes they caused harm to participants who did not consent to and were not informed of what was actually going on throughout the experiment. Oftentimes they caused harm to animals.

Ethical issues that one must consider when doing research include the following:

1. A participant must consent to being in the experiment and must be informed about the purposes, nature and funding for the experiment.

2. A participant is free to opt out of an experiment at any time during the experiment.

3. All details and data collected in the experiment remains anonymous and confidential in nature and is not identifiable.

4. No intentional harm will be done to a participant during an experiment.

5. The results of the experiment are represented accurately by the person/people conducting the experiment.

Unethical Research

Let's look at some well-known unethical psychological experiments.

The Monster Study

The Monster study (1939) concerned an experiment about stuttering carried out on 22 orphans. Two researchers from Iowa, Wendell Johnson and Mary Tudor, separated the orphans into two groups. Each group was a mixture of children without speech problems. The first group received encouragement and positive feedback, while the second group was ridiculed for any speech issues, including non-existent ones. The outcome was that the children in the second group developed speech problems, which they had for the rest of their lives. The study continued for six months and caused lasting, chronic psychological issues. The study was never published.

The Milgram Conformity Experiment

Following the horrors of World War II, the Milgram experiment (1961) was devised by American psychologist Stanley Milgram who wanted to know why ordinary citizens carried out atrocities under the command of Adolf Hitler. Milgram set up an experiment to measure an individual's willingness to obey a person in power. Two participants (one of whom was secretly an actor) were separated in two rooms where they could only hear one another. The test subject then read a series of questions to the actor. Each time the actor gave an incorrect answer, the test subject was ordered to push a button to administer an electric shock. Although many of the test subjects expressed a desire to stop the experiment at the first signs of screams, nearly every one continued to push the button when they were told they would not be held personally responsible for any consequences.

The Stanford Prison Experiment

Perhaps one of the most famous experiments carried out on humans, the Stanford Prison experiment (1971) sought to study the causes of conflict between prisoners and guards. Twenty-four male students were randomly assigned the roles of guard or prisoner and were then set up in their roles in the basement of the psychology building on Stanford University's campus. Quite quickly the guards became aggressive towards the prisoners while the prisoners quite quickly accepted their punishments. The guards became so violent that the experiment had to be ended after just six days.

Apply your learning

Research the three following experiments. Find out how the experiment was conducted, what happened during the experiment and why it is considered unethical.

1 Facial Expressions experiment (1924)
2 Bobo Doll experiment (1961–1963)
3 UCLA Schizophrenic experiments (1983–1994).

Review what you have learned

1. List the four overall ethical principles according to the PSI.
2. List the five ethical issues that one must consider when undertaking research.

chapter 12
WORKING IN PSYCHOLOGY

IN THIS CHAPTER YOU WILL LEARN ABOUT:

- interpersonal skills needed to be an effective caregiver
- healthy boundaries and self-care
- the art of reflection.

Interpersonal Skills

In order to provide effective care, a number of interpersonal skills are needed.

- **Communication:** We can communicate verbally and non-verbally. Positive verbal communication involves speaking in a supportive and non-aggressive way to relay a point. Positive non-verbal communication includes active listening, eye contact, facial expression and body language. Active listening requires you to listen attentively to a client. You may repeat or rephrase to the client what they have said while providing space for the client to speak and be heard. Eye contact, facial expression and body language is used to demonstrate that you are paying attention.

> **Task**
> **Think-Pair-Share**
> Think of ways in which open communication can be blocked by body language. Pair and share your thoughts.

- **Empathy:** Empathy involves perceiving a situation from the other person's point of view. In other words, you put yourself in their shoes and consider the situation from their perspective. By doing this you are less like to be judgemental in your interpretations and interactions.

- **Patience:** Patience is key when working with a client. Each person will progress in their own way and at their own pace. Slowing down your speech and giving time to a client is necessary for them to feel comfortable and relaxed in your presence and in your work together.

- **Kindness:** Kindness is an ingredient that is needed in any successful relationship but crucial to the development of trust and consistency with a client. Kindness does not mean that you become friends with a client – this would be inappropriate. Rather, it refers to showing care and warmth for the person so that they feel enabled to open up to you.

- **Honesty:** Honesty is an integral part of working with any client. A client deserves authenticity in your interactions. It is also important to be honest with your client and with yourself about your own limitations when necessary.

- **Validation:** Validation is something that most clients look for in a therapeutic setting. Acknowledging and hearing how someone feels is a huge part of therapeutic work. Attuning to your client and allowing them to say what they want and feel how they want in the moment without trying to adjust or 'fix' their views or opinions is often as much as is needed in that moment.

- **Self-awareness:** Self-awareness also plays a large role in therapeutic work. It is necessary to set your own boundaries and know your own limits when working with a client. If you are going through personal struggles or experiencing strain that you are not coping with, you need to be aware of these factors and make adjustments so as to manage not only your personal but also your professional life.

- **Creativity:** Having a creative approach is very beneficial in allowing you to think outside the box in terms of how best to assist the client. For example, a client may have a love of music, art, reading or another other creative pursuit that could be used in a therapeutic way to support them holistically.
- **Flexibility:** While it is important to set boundaries in terms of your working hours and schedule (see below), life will often intervene to disrupt plans. It is important to be open to being flexible in your approach to your work and working hours to meet the needs of your clients and work peers.

Healthy Boundaries

The therapist–client relationship is not a friendship. Following ethical guidelines, the therapist has a duty of care to the client who will more often than not present at a vulnerable time in their life seeking help. The therapist must be very clear on the expectations they have both of themselves and their client and communicate these boundaries clearly from the beginning in an honest way.

Here are some examples of unhelpful or inappropriate behaviour in the therapist–client relationship:

- **Giving extra time in a session:** If the session is one hour, then it is an hour that cannot change, even if the client is late to the session. (However, as mentioned above, a certain degree of flexibility might be necessary depending on the situation and at the discretion of the therapist.)
- **Therapist oversharing:** The therapist should not discuss their own issues with a client – as well as being inappropriate, it takes time out of their session. The session is about them and not you.

- **Speaking about a client outside of a session:** The therapist must not speak to anyone else about a client or the content of their sessions. It is advisable that all therapists receive therapy themselves to process their work or deal with any arising issues. In doing so, the therapist can speak about their work in a confidential manner, anonymising the client if need be.

- **Starting another type of relationship with a client:** It is highly inappropriate and unethical to enter into a relationship, particularly a romantic relationship, with a client. If romantic feelings for a client arise, it is part of the therapist's duty of care to transfer the client to another therapist. Similarly, having a friendship outside of therapy with a client is entirely inappropriate. It is also inadvisable to act as a therapist for family members, friends or friends of friends.

Remember that if you are uncomfortable with any client behaviour, you should reflect on it in your own therapy work and make arrangements to discuss the issue with the client if necessary and at an appropriate time.

Self-Care

Everyone experiences issues and stresses in life. Being a therapist does not mean being immune to life's problems. In order to maintain a healthy professional life and avoid burnout while enjoying a fulfilling and satisfying personal life, it is necessary to strike a balance and maintain a separation between both. To this end, and for the sake of your own mental and physical wellbeing, it is very important to practise self-care.

- Adhering to strict work hours helps you to keep your personal time for yourself, your family and friends.

- Having a work phone and work computer makes it easier to keep things separate.

- Finding ways every day to unwind and destress can be helpful, while carving out dedicated time to exercise, socialise with family, cook dinner, meditate or do some other activities that help you to restore your balance will help to prevent burnout in your profession.

Everyone will have a different self-care routine. The important thing to note is that it is a practice or routine that needs to be repeated frequently to get results.

Here is a sample self-care routine.

Day	Morning	Evening
Monday	Meditate 10 minutes	Go for a walk in the park
Wednesday	Gratitude journaling 10 minutes	Read a good book (put phone on silent)
Friday	Yoga 15 minutes	Meet up with friends for dinner
Sunday	Cup of tea and sit in the garden	Take a bath

Reflection

Reflection and having the time and space to think critically and learn from events and situations that arise in your life is an invaluable tool for your own personal and academic learning, growth and development. Having a time and space to journal your thoughts and feelings daily or weekly – especially if you are in a therapeutic role – will allow you to process events or learning and understand yourself more fully.

Gibbs' Reflective Cycle

Gibbs' Reflective Cycle (1988) is just one of many approaches to the reflective process. Within this process, the practitioner asks themselves the following questions:

1. Describe what happened.
2. How did you feel and think?
3. Was it good or bad?
4. What was the learning?
5. What else could you have done?
6. What would you do differently if it happened again?

WORKING IN PSYCHOLOGY

Apply your learning

Read the following case study. Write up in brief:

1 The interpersonal skills you would need when working with this client
2 The advice you would offer this client.

Case study: Kate

Kate is a fifth-year student. She is captain of her hockey team and also has a part-time job in the local supermarket. Kate has just recently had her first kiss and is getting closer to her new boyfriend, Matthew. This has put a strain on her friendship with Chloe, her best friend. Chloe has recently started hanging out with another group of girls from another school that Kate doesn't know. Kate misses her friend. She is also uncomfortable with the speed at which things are progressing with Matthew.

Kate is in the following stages:

+ **Erikson stage: 5**
  In this stage Kate is questioning where she fits in and belongs. Her peer group may be of great importance to her as well. On a social level, adolescents are very influenced by youth culture as they begin to focus more on their peer group and their social and emotional life outside of the home.

+ **Piaget stage: Formal operational**
  At this point in Kate's development, thinking becomes much more sophisticated and advanced. Skills such as logical thought, deductive reasoning and systematic planning also emerge during this stage. Moral reasoning also emerges.

+ **Freud stage: Genital**
  In this stage Kate might be engaging in sexual experimentation.

+ Lifespan/biological stage: Adolescence
In this stage, on a biological level, Kate is undergoing physical changes in the body internally and externally, leading to the development of hips and breasts and the possible onset of acne. On a social level, Kate might be engaging in risk-taking behaviour, developing interest in intimacy and in sexual relationships.

Review what you have learned

1. List and describe three interpersonal skills needed when working with any client.
2. Explain why it is necessary to have boundaries in a healthy relationship.
3. Explain the purpose of reflection in psychology.

chapter 13
CASE STUDIES

> **Note:** All case studies feature a fictitious person. No real names or details have been provided.

When assessing the needs of a client and how these needs can be met, various theories can be used. The following case study provides an example of how the theories of Maslow's Hierarchy of Needs and Bronfenbrenner's ecological systems can be used in analysis and intervention as well as the interpersonal skills needed.

Case study: Gemma

You are a case worker employed by a statutory organisation funded by the Department of Education and Skills whose aim is to improve school retention rates. You have been asked by Gemma's principal to consult with the people closest to Gemma with the aim of improving Gemma's school experience.

Gemma is a six-year-old girl living in Laois. Two months ago her mum had a second child, a baby boy named Luke. Her dad works full-time in the bank and last year started travelling overseas from time to time. Her mum is currently on maternity leave from her full-time job in the IT sector.

For the last three months, Gemma has begun to express an unwillingness to go to school. In the morning she hides from her mother. She has also had problems sleeping and is waking up during the night at times and going into her mum's room. She spends an hour each morning sitting outside her classroom refusing to go in and has recently hit and bitten one of her peers after entering the class. Her friend Áine has now made a new best friend. After entering the classroom and settling down, no further incidents happen during the day.

Before the onset of this behaviour, Gemma enjoyed school. She is very creative. She has missed more and more school in the last three months and her teacher is concerned about these changes. In addition to this, Gemma is on a waiting list through the HSE to be assessed for psychological support.

Needs Analysis

Having consulted with Gemma's family and Gemma herself, the following needs analysis chart was filled in, based on Maslow's Hierarchy of Needs.

Level of need	Being met +	Not being met -
Physiological needs	Food, clothing, water, shelter	Sleep
Safety needs	Care of family, safe neighbourhood	Lack of emotional support from parents may be leading Gemma to feel unsafe emotionally
Love and belonging	Parental involvement	Doesn't feel like she belongs due to arrival of new baby
Esteem	Is still engaging in school and seems to want to re-engage with friends	Lost friendship Missing school
Self-actualisation	Has a love of creativity	Can't actualise fully

Needs Intervention

Here are suggested interventions for those unmet needs using Bronfenbrenner's ecological systems theory.

Psychology perspective	Microsystem	Mesosystem	Exosystem (may not relate to perspective)	Macrosystem (may not relate to perspective)
Psycho-analysis	Psycho-analytic play therapy	Family talk therapy	Mum could get help with Luke to have more one-on-one time with Gemma	The Aistear curriculum supports, which allow the child to lead and have a voice. Using creativity throughout the school curriculum, which allows the child to express themselves through play and art
Behaviourism	Counter-conditioning for attending school	Operant conditioning – teacher and parents could create a rewards system for when Gemma enters the classroom	Mum and Dad could spend more time with Gemma as a reward for positive behaviour	

Psychology perspective	Microsystem	Mesosystem	Exosystem (may not relate to perspective)	Macrosystem (may not relate to perspective)
Cognitive	CBT	Family CBT	Dad could restructure work life	SilverCloud Health (online platform)
Humanistic	Integrative play therapy	In integrative play therapy the family is also involved and must attend the first and last session	Nature walks in a local park	Creative mindfulness (https://www.creative-mindfulness.com)

Interpersonal Skills Needed

+ communication: active listening
+ empathy
+ patience
+ kindness
+ creative approach to helping with anxiety.

Apply your learning

You are working with Foróige Youth Service and the Department of Education and Skills in a new initiative to support students academically and holistically. You will be liaising with the following clients and their support networks to assist them in dealing with the issues being presented. Apply what you have learned to assess your clients' needs and identify possible interventions.

Case 1: Exam pressure/Self-esteem issues

Nathan is a 17-year-old adolescent who lives in Tallaght, Dublin, with his mother and two younger sisters. Nathan will be sitting his Leaving Cert exams this year. He has a part-time job in McDonald's to help his mother out with the bills. In school, Nathan is quiet but is liked by teachers and peers. He has a close group of three male friends. His aunt is supportive and has been helping him with honours maths and watching his two sisters while he studies, as his mum works nights. His sisters are very proud of him and look up to him, and he wants to make them and his mum proud.

Nathan has been under a lot of stress this academic year juggling work and study. He has stopped going to football practice. His friends seem to have grown distant. He is also concerned about weight gain and acne. His mock exams are coming up soon and he feels unprepared.

1 Assess whether Nathan's level of need is being met.

Level of need	Being met +	Not being met -
Physiological needs		
Safety needs		
Love and belonging		
Esteem		
Self-actualisation		

2 Identify interventions for needs not being met.

Psychology perspective	Microsystem	Mesosystem	Exosystem (may not relate to perspective)	Macrosystem (may not relate to perspective)

Case 2: Emotional turmoil

Joanne is a 16-year-old adolescent living in Limerick city. Joanne lives with her 10-year-old twin siblings and her grandparents. Recently her uncle has been helping the family out with school drop-off and has been helping Joanne with schoolwork as she has been struggling with maths and science. However, when he is helping Joanne, he often comments on her clothes, weight and hair, saying things such as, 'Why don't you try to lose some weight and get a boyfriend?' He thinks he is being helpful, but this makes Joanne feel very uncomfortable. Her siblings have heard these comments and are now also asking Joanne why she doesn't have a boyfriend. Joanne is finding this very difficult to deal with.

1 Assess whether Joanne's level of need is being met.

Level of need	Being met +	Not being met -
Physiological needs		
Safety needs		
Love and belonging		
Esteem		
Self-actualisation		

2 Identify interventions for needs not being met.

Psychology perspective	Microsystem	Mesosystem	Exosystem (may not relate to perspective)	Macrosystem (may not relate to perspective)

CASE STUDIES

Case 3: School stress/Mental health

Sam is a 15-year-old adolescent living in Galway. He is doing the Junior Certificate this year. He enjoys the practical subjects and likes hands-on projects but is not academically inclined. Since he has started secondary school, he has struggled to keep the same group of friends as they do not have the same interests. Last year his parents split up, and he now rarely sees his father. He helps a lot at home with his younger siblings as his mother works two jobs, so he does not have a lot of free time. Sam is struggling in school. He needs advice on whether to continue school or go into a trade but has no one to turn to as he feels his mum is too busy to bother and his father hasn't been answering his calls or messages in recent months.

1. Assess whether Sam's level of need is being met.

Level of need	Being met +	Not being met -
Physiological needs		
Safety needs		
Love and belonging		
Esteem		
Self-actualisation		

2   Identify interventions for needs not being met.

Psychology perspective	Microsystem	Mesosystem	Exosystem (may not relate to perspective)	Macrosystem (may not relate to perspective)

chapter 14
EXAM QUESTIONS WITH ANSWERS

Sample Exam Paper 1

Ten short questions (2 marks each). Answer all ten questions.

1 Name four different perspectives of psychology.

2 Identify two limitations of Piaget's stages of cognitive development.

3 Explain the term 'operant conditioning'. Give one example.

4 Who is known as the father of attachment theory?

5 Define 'cognitive psychology'.

6 Draw and label the zone of proximal development.

7 Name two theorists in psychoanalytic psychology.

8 Identify the three parenting styles, according to Baumrind.

9 Name the three parts of the mind, according to Freud.

10 Draw and label Maslow's Hierarchy of Needs.

Three long questions (10 marks each). Answer two.

Question 1:

(a) Draw and describe an ecosystem model for a six-year-old child. (8 marks – 4 marks for correctly labelled drawing; 4 marks for description of each part of model)

(b) Who developed ecological systems theory? (2 marks)

Question 2:

(a) What is a defence mechanism? (2 marks)

(b) Who created the concept? (2 marks)

(c) From what field of psychology does this work come? (2 marks)

(d) List and describe four defence mechanisms. (4 marks)

Question 3:

(a) What is meant by cognition? (2 marks)

(b) How can CBT improve a person's life? (2 marks)

(c) What is cognitive distortion? (2 marks)

(d) List and describe four cognitive distortions. (4 marks)

Sample Exam Paper 2

Ten short questions (2 marks each). Answer all ten questions.

1. What does CBT stand for?

2. What type of psychologist was Diana Baumrind?

3. How many stages are there in Piaget's theory of cognitive development?

4. What information can be accessed in DSM-V?

5. What is an archetype, according to Carl Jung?

6. List three defence mechanisms, according to Freud.

7. What perspective of psychology does transpersonal therapy stem from?

8. What is the CNS and what does it do?

9. Name one type of drug used to treat depression.

10. What are the 'four Ds' in relation to abnormal behaviour?

EXAM QUESTIONS WITH ANSWERS

Three long questions (10 marks each). Answer two.

Question 1:

Outline the work of Mary Ainsworth, including the steps in the 'Strange Situation' experiment and the findings that came from that experiment.

Question 2:

Describe Stage 5 of Erik Erikson's psychosocial development theory, Identity versus Role Confusion, outlining the challenges the adolescent faces in this stage and some tools that could help them negotiate the stage successfully.

Question 3:

(a) Outline the four overall ethical principles according to the PSI Code of Professional Ethics.

(b) Describe one unethical psychological experiment and state the principles that it did not uphold.

Sample Exam Paper 1 – Answers

Ten short questions (2 marks each)

1. Name four different perspectives of psychology.

   For example: Psychodynamic/Behavioural/Cognitive/Humanistic/Biological.

2. Identify two limitations of Piaget's stages of cognitive development.

   1. It does not account for the environment the child is in.

   2. It was based on observations of his own children so it's possibly subjective.

3. Explain the term 'operant conditioning'. Give one example.

   Operant conditioning is conditioning where you apply a positive reinforcement to increase a certain behaviour. For example, a teacher gives a child a gold star every time they do their homework, therefore increasing the number of times they turn in homework.

4. Who is known as the father of attachment theory?

   John Bowlby.

5. Define 'cognitive psychology'.

   Cognitive psychology is defined as the study of the mind and how it processes information.

6. Draw and label the zone of proximal development.

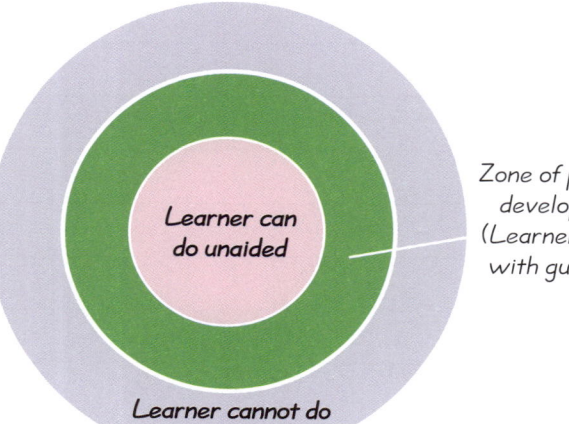

7 Name two theorists in psychoanalytic psychology.

For example: Sigmund Freud/Anna Freud/Carl Jung/John Bowlby/ Erik Erikson.

8 What are the three parenting styles, according to Baumrind?

Authoritarian, authoritative and permissive.

9 Name the three parts of the mind, according to Freud.

Id, ego and superego.

10 Draw and label Maslow's Hierarchy of Needs.

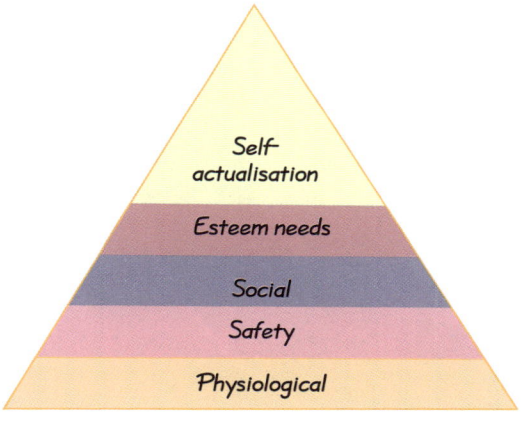

Three long questions (10 marks each).

Question 1:

(a) Draw and describe an ecosystem model for a six-year-old child.

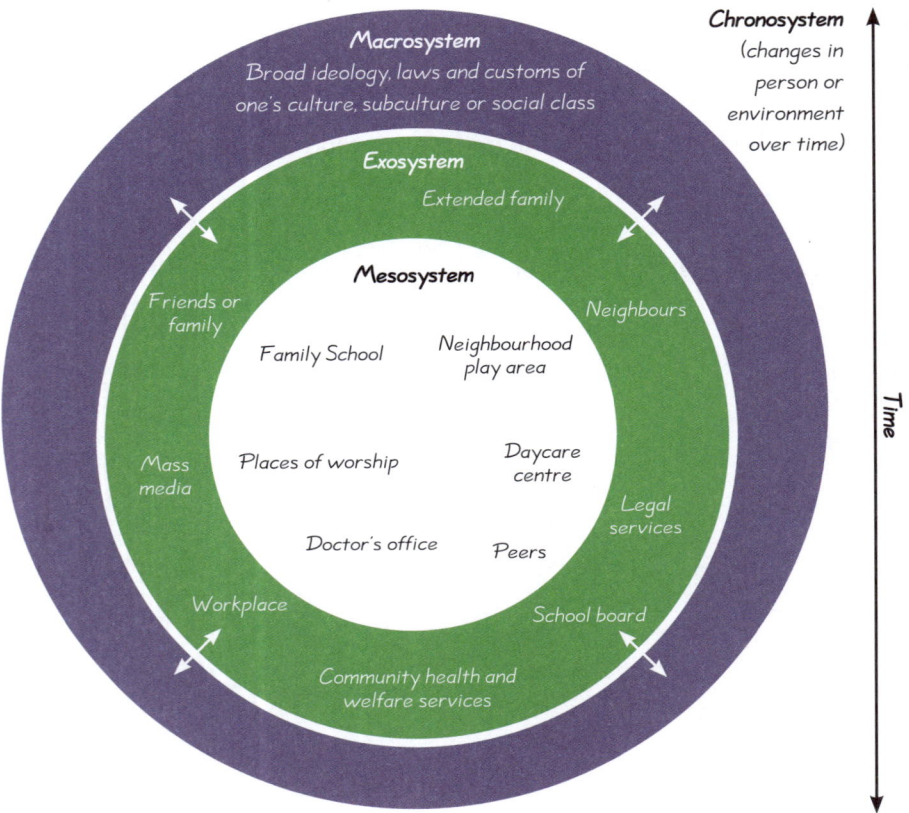

(b) Who developed ecological systems theory?

Urie Bronfenbrenner.

Question 2:

(a) What is a defence mechanism?

Defence mechanisms are psychological strategies that are unconsciously used to protect a person from anxiety arising from unacceptable thoughts or feelings.

(b) Who created the concept?

Sigmund Freud.

(c) From what field of psychology does this work come?

Psychoanalysis.

(d) List and describe four defence mechanisms.

For example:

Repression: Used to prevent disturbing or threatening thoughts from becoming conscious. Involves forcing disturbing thoughts or ideas into the unconscious, where, although hidden, they will create anxiety.

Denial: Blocking external events from awareness, so that the person refuses to experience it.

Projection: When an individual projects their own unacceptable or unpleasant thoughts on to another person.

Displacement: Satisfying an impulse with a substitute object. If someone is frustrated by their superiors, they may take their anger out on an object or person.

Regression: Moving back in time psychologically when faced with stress. A child may begin to suck their thumb again when they need to spend time in the hospital.

Sublimation: Using a socially acceptable substitute object to satisfy an impulse, e.g. sports.

Rationalisation: The distortion of 'facts' to make an event or an impulse less threatening. We do this when we provide ourselves with excuses. As we are never truly aware of it, many of us are quite prepared to believe our own lies.

Question 3:

(a) What is meant by cognition?

Cognition is the concept that your brain is an information processing system that deals with the areas of memory, learning and emotions.

(b) How can CBT improve a person's life?

CBT can improve a person's life by helping them to reframe unhealthy or negative thoughts or beliefs into more healthy positive beliefs. This allows them to overcome negative behaviour and thought patterns that may be causing anxiety, stress, depression, etc.

(c) What is cognitive distortion?

A cognitive distortion is an error in logic that causes inaccurate thoughts or feelings.

(d) List and describe four cognitive distortions.

For example:
Jumping to conclusions: Where one judges or decides something without having all the facts.

Over-generalisation: Where a single event is viewed as an invariable rule.

Black-and-white thinking: A thought pattern that makes people think in absolutes.

Catastrophising: Assuming the worst will happen.

Sample Exam Paper 2 – Answers

Ten short questions (2 marks each)

1. What does CBT stand for?

   Cognitive Behavioural Therapy.

2. What type of psychologist was Diana Baumrind?

   She was a developmental psychologist who studied parenting styles.

3. How many stages are there in Piaget's theory of cognitive development?

   There are four stages: sensorimotor, preoperational, concrete operational and formal operational.

4. What information can be accessed in DSM-V?

   DSM-V lists categories of mental disorders along with some related disorders. There are currently 157 disorders listed in this DSM.

5. What is an archetype, according to Carl Jung?

   According to Carl Jung, an archetype is a theme or image that comes from the collective and has common meanings across cultures.

6. List three defence mechanisms, according to Freud.

   Repression, regression and sublimation.

7. What perspective of psychology does transpersonal therapy stem from?

   It stems from humanistic psychology.

8. What is the CNS and what does it do?

   The CNS is the central nervous system. It is the central power station of the body, the brain being the command centre and the spinal cord sending messages to and from the brain to the peripheral nervous system.

9 Name one type of drug used to treat depression.

For example: Zoloft/Paxil/Prozac.

10 What are the 'four Ds' in relation to abnormal behaviour?

Dysfunction, distress, deviancy, danger.

Three long questions (10 marks each)

Question 1:

Outline the work of Mary Ainsworth, including the steps in the 'Strange Situation' experiment and the findings that came from that experiment.

This experiment was based around infants aged 12 to 18 months and attempted to explore the interactions between them, their mother and a stranger to ascertain whether or not the infant would exhibit separation anxiety when not in the presence of the mother/when in the presence of a stranger.

- *The mother and child are brought into a room and allowed to settle for one minute.*
- *The mother and child play together with toys for three minutes.*
- *The stranger enters the room and sits down quietly for one minute, chats to the mother for one minute and then plays with the child for one minute.*
- *The mother then says goodbye to the child and leaves the room for three minutes.*
- *The mother then returns and the stranger leaves. The mother offers herself as a comfort to the child (e.g. by holding out her arms) if the child seeks comforting.*
- *The mother leaves again and the child is left alone for three minutes.*
- *The stranger returns and comforts the child if the child seeks comforting.*

- After three minutes, the mother returns and the stranger leaves. Again the mother offers herself as a comfort to the child if the child seeks comforting.

Ainsworth and her researchers analysed the reunion phase and, looking for certain behaviours, observed and scored infants. From their findings they identified four distinctive attachment styles.

1 Secure attachment: Sixty-five to 70 per cent of infants were in this category. These infants were more likely to cry when the mother left the room and were less likely to be calmed down by the stranger. They were calmed down by their mother when she returned and appeared to be happy and trusting of the comfort their mother gave them. When they were calm they were able to return to play with the toys once again.

2 Insecure-avoidant attachment: Ten to 15 per cent of infants were in this category. These children were not as likely to be upset when their mother left the room and when she re-entered the room did not usually look for her to comfort them. They were more receptive to the stranger than securely attached children, even when alone with the stranger.

3 Insecure-resistant attachment: Fifteen to 20 per cent of infants were in this category. They cried a lot when the mother left the room. However, when the mother re-entered the room, they were resistant and did not always seek comfort from her. Even if they did seek comfort they were not always reassured by the mother and often continued to be upset for longer than securely attached children.

4 Disorganised attachment: About five per cent of infants were in this category. Some were upset when the mother left the room and some were not. When the mother re-entered the room they were not sure exactly what to do and exhibited mixed responses to the mother, either resisting and then avoiding or avoiding and then resisting. In follow-ups, this group of children seemed to fare the worst in life.

Question 2:

Describe Stage 5 of Erik Erikson's psychosocial development theory, Identity versus Role Confusion, outlining the challenges the adolescent faces in this stage and some tools that could help them negotiate the stage successfully.

Peer relationships are a major focus at this stage, with adolescents seeking peer approval. A young person usually moves away from family relationships and focuses more on friendships through school or involvement in sports, work or other interests. Peer relationships can play a positive or negative role in the development of a young person during this stage. A young person will seek to find their own identity and will explore different elements of youth culture such as music, clothing, hairstyles, personal appearance and so on. A young person may engage in risky behaviour, e.g. alcohol or drug use or other adventure-seeking behaviour. Sometimes they may feel pressured by peers to fit in and belong. A young person who understands that it is normal to feel self-conscious and to question their identity at this stage will have more compassion and empathy for themselves. If they have good friends and people with whom they can talk, and if they can engage in self-care, including a healthy diet, daily exercise and other positive outlets for stress and peer pressure, they will have a great chance of finding their own identity separate from peer and family groups.

Question 3:

(a) Outline the four overall ethical principles according to the PSI Code of Professional Ethics.

   The four overall ethical principles according to the PSI Code of Professional Ethics are:

   Principle 1 *Respect for the rights and dignity of the person*
   This principle requires of psychologists that they treat their clients as persons of intrinsic worth with a right to determine their own priorities, that they respect clients' dignity, and give due regard to their moral and cultural values.

Principle 2 *Competence*
Psychologists must maintain and update their professional skills and ethical awareness. They shall recognise that psychological knowledge and their own expertise and capacity for work are limited, and take care not to exceed the limits.

Principle 3 *Responsibility*
Psychologists are required to act in a trustworthy, reputable and accountable manner towards clients and the community. They shall avoid doing harm to clients and research participants, and act to prevent harm caused by others. They shall cooperate with colleagues and other professionals to ensure the best service to clients, and act positively to resolve ethical dilemmas. They shall ensure that those whom they supervise act ethically. In research with animals, they shall take care to treat the animals humanely.

Principle 4 *Integrity*
Psychologists are obliged to be honest and accurate about their qualifications, the effectiveness of the services which they offer, and their research findings. They shall take steps to manage personal stress and maintain their own mental health. They shall treat others in a fair, open and straightforward manner, honour professional commitments and act to clarify any confusion about their role or responsibilities.

(b) Describe one unethical psychological experiment and state the principles that it did not uphold.

In this case of Baby Albert, the experiment was unethical because:

1. After the experimenter found out that baby Albert had a medical condition they continued with the experiment. Here the principles of respect, responsibility and integrity were broken.

2. The experiment was set up to examine classical conditioning in humans but only one subject, a white male baby under one year, was used to examine this. Here the principle of integrity was broken.

3. This experiment is difficult to replicate as the researchers did not explain or outline how they collected their data. Again the principles of integrity and responsibility were broken.

GLOSSARY OF TERMS

Accommodation the process of creating a new folder or schema or changing schema when presented with new information (Piaget)

Amygdala a part of the brain involved in memory and emotional processes

Anal compulsive a pattern of behaviour whereby a strong need and compulsion to organise, clean and keep everything in order exists (Freud)

Anal expulsive a pattern of behaviour where a person lacks organisation (Freud)

Anima the ideal woman in a man's psyche, represents femininity (Jung)

Animus the ideal man in the woman's psyche, represents masculinity (Jung)

Archetype a concept describing universal knowledge and ideals passed down from ancestors and held in the collective unconscious (Jung)

Assimilation the process of taking in new or similar information into already existing schema (Piaget)

Aversion therapy using something unpleasant to stop an undesirable behaviour

Behaviourism the concept that all behaviours are acquired through conditioning, and conditioning occurs through interaction with the environment

Broca's area	an area of the brain in the frontal lobe that is involved with speech production
Catharsis	the process of releasing, and thereby providing relief from, strong or repressed emotions
Causation	the action of causing something
CBT	Cognitive Behavioural Therapy; a step-by-step process to treat negative thoughts and assumptions (Ellis/Beck)
Classical conditioning	a process of learning by association (Pavlov/Watson)
Collective unconscious	the repressed thoughts, feelings and emotions of the collective (Jung)
Congruence	a state of being in balance as a person (Rogers)
Consciousness	a subjective awareness of your thoughts and feelings and the world around you
Correlation	the degree to which two variables move in the same direction as each other
Defence mechanism	a psychological strategy used to ward off unpleasant thoughts or feelings (Freud)
DNA	deoxyribonucleic acid; a molecule that contains the biological instructions that make each species unique
Dream analysis	therapeutic technique used to uncover the hidden meanings in dreams through analysing a series of symbols (Freud)
DSM	*The Diagnostic and Statistical Manual*; a handbook used mainly in the USA for the diagnosis of mental health disorders

GLOSSARY OF TERMS

Ego — the part of the personality that mediates between the id and the superego, concerned with the reality principle (Freud); everything that creates consciousness – all of the unrepressed thoughts, feelings and emotions of a person (Jung)

Electra complex — a psychoanalytic term used to describe a girl's sense of competition with her mother for the affections of her father (Freud)

Erogenous zone — a sensitive area on the body that causes sexual arousal when it is touched (Freud)

Ethics — the moral principles that govern a person's behaviour

Extinction — (in classical conditioning) the ending of the learned or conditioned response after a period of time when the unconditioned stimulus is no longer presented alongside the conditioned stimulus

Extrovert — an outgoing, socially confident person, whose attention is directed towards other people and the outside world (Jung)

Fixation — the idea that part of a person's libido is stuck in a particular stage of development because of overindulgence or a blockage (Freud)

Free association — a therapeutic technique whereby a client is asked to think and talk freely about whatever comes to mind as regards a situation, topic or person (Freud)

Freudian slip — an unintentional error regarded as revealing subconscious feelings (Freud)

Genetics	a branch of biology that studies heredity and genes
Humanistic psychology	psychological perspective that emphasises the person as a unique individual and focuses on meeting the holistic needs of each individual
Hypothalamus	a small area at the base of the brain involved in controlling appetite, hormone secretion and production and regulating processes such as temperature, emotions and other physiological cycles
Hypothesis	a proposed explanation for something with limited evidence as a basis for further investigation
Id	the part of personality concerned with basic needs and drives (Freud)
Incongruence	a state of being out of balance as a person (Rogers)
Introvert	a shy, reticent person whose interest is generally directed inward towards his own feelings and thoughts (Jung)
Libido	sexual energy created through different types of behaviours (Freud)
MKO	'more knowledgeable other', relating to the zone of proximal development (Vygotsky)
Monotropy	a term relating to the single strong attachment that happens from birth with a child and their mother or fundamental carer (Bowlby)
Neuron	the fundamental units of the brain and nervous system, the cells responsible for receiving sensory input from the external world, for

GLOSSARY OF TERMS

	sending motor commands to our muscles, and for transforming and relaying the electrical signals at every step in between
Neurotransmitter	chemical messengers used to transmit messages from one neuron to the next neuron
Oedipus complex	a psychoanalytic term used to describe a boy's sense of competition with his father for the affections of his mother (Freud)
Operant conditioning	learning through a system of rewards or punishments for behaviour (Skinner)
Personal unconscious	the repressed thoughts, feelings and emotions of a person (Jung)
Pineal gland	a pea-size gland in the brain involved in melatonin secretion and conveying light and dark cycles from the environment to the brain
Pituitary gland	a small gland at the base of the brain involved in hormone production
Qualitative data	deals with words and ideas
Quantitative data	deals with numbers
REBT	Rational Emotive Behavioural Therapy, the first form of CBT (Ellis)
Schema	a cognitive term describing a category of knowledge that helps us to understand and interpret the world (Piaget)
Self-actualisation	the full development and realisation of one's abilities (Rogers)
Self-concept	how you perceive your abilities and unique characteristics (Rogers)

Superego	the part of the personality concerned with the conscience, driven by morals and what is considered right and wrong (Freud)
Teratogen	any agent that can do harm to the foetus during pregnancy such as alcohol, drugs or smoking
Transference	a redirection of feelings from one person to someone else
Unconditional positive regard	having acceptance of and giving support to a person regardless of whether one is in agreement with them
Unconditioned response	(in classical conditioning) the automatic or unlearned reaction to an unconditioned stimulus; for example, the reaction to the smell of food when hungry is to salivate
Unconditioned stimulus	(in classical conditioning) something in the environment that causes an automatic response; for example, the smell of food when one is hungry is an unconditioned stimulus
Variable	anything that is liable to change and that can be measured, for example, age
Wernicke's area	a region of the brain involved in the comprehension of speech

BIBLIOGRAPHY

American Psychiatric Association (2013) *Diagnostic and Statistical Manual of Mental Disorders*, 5th edition. Arlington, VA: American Psychiatric Association.

Amiel Castro, R., Glover, V., Ehlert, U. and O'Connor, T. (2021) 'Breastfeeding. Prenatal Depression and Children's IQ and Behaviour: A Test of a Moderation Model'. In: *BMC Pregnancy and Childbirth*, 21(62). Available from: https://doi.org/10.1186/s12884-020-03520-8 [accessed 9 March 2022].

Asch, S.E. (1952) 'Effects of Group Pressure on the Modification and Distortion of Judgments'. In: H. Guetzkow (ed.), *Groups, Leadership and Men*. Pittsburgh, PA: Carnegie Press, pp. 177–90.

Baumrind, D. (2013) 'Authoritative Parenting Revisited: History and Current Status'. In R.E. Larzelere, A. Sheffield and A. W. Harrist (eds.), *Authoritative Parenting: Synthesising Nurturance and Discipline for Optimal Child Development*. Washington, DC: American Psychological Association, pp. 11–34.

— (1991) 'Parenting Styles and Adolescent Development'. In J. Brooks-Gurn, R.M. Lerner and A.C. Petersen (eds.), *The Encyclopedia on Adolescence*. New York: Garland Publishing, pp. 746–58.

— (1991) 'The Influence of Parenting Style on Adolescent Competence and Substance Use'. In: *Journal of Early Adolescence*, 11(1), pp. 56–95.

Beck, A.T. (1963) 'Thinking and Depression: I. Idiosyncratic Content and Cognitive Distortions'. In: *Archives of General Psychiatry*, 9(4), pp. 324–33.

— (1967) *Depression: Causes and Treatment*. Philadelphia: University of Pennsylvania Press.

— (1976) *Cognitive Therapy and Emotional Disorders*. Oxford: International Universities Press.

Beck, A.T., Rush, A.J., Shaw, B.F., Emery, G. (1979) *Cognitive Therapy of Depression*. New York: Guilford Press.

Beck, K. (2019) 'Law of Independent Assortment (Mendel): Definition, Explanation, Example'. Available from: https://sciencing.com/law-of-independent-assortment-mendel-definition-explanation-example-13718436.html [accessed 9 March 2022].

Bowlby, J. (1944) 'Forty-Four Juvenile Thieves: Their Characters and Home Life'. In: *International Journal of Psychoanalysis*, 25(19–52), pp. 107–27.

— (1952) 'Maternal Care and Mental Health'. In: *Journal of Consulting Psychology*, 16(3), p. 232.

— (1953) *Child Care and the Growth of Love*. London: Penguin Books.

— (1956) 'Mother-Child Separation'. In: *Mental Health and Infant Development*, 1, pp. 117–22.

— (1968) *Attachment and Loss, Vol. 1: Attachment*. New York: Basic Books.

— (1973) *Attachment and Loss, Vol. 2: Separation, Anxiety, and Anger*. New York: Basic Books.

— (1980) *Attachment and Loss, Vol. 3: Loss, Sadness and Depression*. New York: Basic Books.

Brewer, C.L. (1991) 'Perspectives on John B. Watson'. In: G.A. Kimble, M. Wertheimer & C. White (eds.), *Portraits of Pioneers in Psychology*. Washington, DC: American Psychological Association, pp. 171–86.

Clark, D.A. and Beck, A.T. (2010) *Cognitive Therapy of Anxiety Disorders: Science and Practice*. New York: Guilford Press.

Chomsky, N. (1959) 'Review of B.F. Skinner's Verbal Behaviour'. In: *Language*, 35, pp. 26–58.

Darwin, C. (1859) *On the Origin of Species by Means of Natural Selection, or the Preservation of Favoured Races in the Struggle for Life*, 1st edition. London: John Murray.

Dasen, P. (1994) 'Culture and Cognitive Development from a Piagetian Perspective'. In: W.J. Lonner and R.S. Malpass (eds.), *Psychology and Culture*. Boston: Allyn and Bacon, pp. 145–9.

Davis, T. (2009) 'Conceptualising Psychiatric Disorders Using "Four D's" of Diagnoses'. Available from: https://www.semanticscholar.org/paper/Conceptualizing-Psychiatric-Disorders-Using-%E2%80%9CFour-Davis/22f9c263d9e69062f8103d5aa8a452ecd94a9705#citing-papers [accessed 9 March 2022].

Drew, T., Võ, M. L-H., Wolfe, J.M. (2013) 'The Invisible Gorilla Strikes Again: Sustained Inattentional Blindness in Expert Observers'. In: *Psychological Science*, 24(9), pp. 1848–53.

Eagly, A.H. and Chaiken, S. (1993) *The Psychology of Attitudes*. CA: Harcourt Brace Jovanovich College Publishers.

Elkind, D. (1967) 'Egocentrism in Adolescence'. In: *Child Development*, 38, pp. 1025–34.

Ellis, A. (1957) 'Rational Psychotherapy and Individual Psychology'. In: *Journal of Individual Psychology*, 13, pp. 38–44.

— (1962) *Reason and Emotion in Psychotherapy*. New York: Stuart.

Freud, A. (1937) *The Ego and the Mechanisms of Defence*. London: Hogarth Press and Institute of Psycho-Analysis.

— (1966) *Normality and Pathology in Childhood: Assessments of Development*. New York: International Universities Press, Inc.

— (1971) *Problems of Psychoanalytic Training, Diagnosis, and the Technique of Therapy, 1966–1970*, Vol. 7. New York: International Universities Press, Inc.

— (1982) *Psychoanalytic Psychology of Normal Development, 1970–1980*. No. 112. London: The Hogarth Press.

Freud, S. (1894) 'The Neuro-Psychoses of Defence'. In: *Standard Edition of the Complete Psychological Works of Sigmund Freud*, Vol. III, pp. 41–61.

— (1896) 'Further Remarks on the Neuro-Psychoses of Defence. In: *Standard Edition* Vol. III, pp. 157–85.

— (1900) 'The Interpretation of Dreams'. In: *Standard Edition* Vol. IV, pp. 4–5.

— (1905) 'Three Essays on the Theory of Sexuality'. In: *Standard Edition* Vol. VII, pp. 123–246.

— (1915) 'The Unconscious'. In: *Standard Edition* Vol. XIV, pp. 159–204.

— (1920) 'Beyond the pleasure principle'. In: *Standard Edition* Vol. XVIII, pp. 1–64.

— (1923) 'The Ego and the Id'. In: *Standard Edition* Vol. XIX, pp. 1–66.

— (1925) 'Negation'. In: *Standard Edition* Vol. XIX, pp. 235–9.

— (1961) 'The Resistances to Psycho-Analysis'. In: *Standard Edition* Vol. XIX, pp. 211–224.

Freud, S. and Breuer. J. (1895) 'Studies on Hysteria'. In: *Standard Edition* Vol. II, pp. 1–335.

Gibbs G. (1988) *Learning by Doing: A Guide to Teaching and Learning Methods*. Oxford: Further Education Unit/Oxford Polytechnic.

Gray, P. (2011) *Psychology*, 6th edition. New York: Worth Publishers.

Greenfield, P.M. (1966) 'On Culture and Conservation'. In: J.S. Bruner *et al.* (eds.) *Studies in Cognitive Growth*. New York: John Wiley, pp. 225–56.

Harlow, H.F., Dodsworth, R.O. and Harlow, M. K. (1965) 'Total Social Isolation in Monkeys'. In: *Proceedings of the National Academy of Sciences of the United States of America*, 54(1), p. 90.

Harlow, H.F. and Zimmermann, R.R. (1958) 'The Development of Affective Responsiveness in Infant Monkeys. In: *Proceedings of the American Philosophical Society*, 102(5), pp. 501–9.

Harlow, J.M. (1848) 'Passage of an Iron Rod through the Head'. In: *Boston Medical and Surgical Journal*, 39, pp. 389–93.

Harris, B. (1979) 'Whatever Happened to Little Albert?' In: *American Psychologist*, 34(2), p. 151.

Holmes, J. (1993) *John Bowlby and Attachment Theory*. London: Routledge.

Hull, C.L. (1935) 'The Conflicting Psychologies of Learning – A Way Out'. In: *Psychological Review*, 42(6), p. 491.

Jung, C.G. (1921) *Psychological Types. The Collected Works of C.G. Jung*, Vol. 6 Bollingen Series XX.

— (1923) 'On the Relation of Analytical Psychology to Poetic Art'. In: *British Journal of Medical Psychology*, 3(3), pp. 213–31.

— (1928) *Contributions to Analytical Psychology*. New York: Harcourt Brace.

— (1933) *Modern Man in Search of His Soul*. London: Kegan Paul, Trench, Trubner and Co.

— (1933) 'The Meaning of Psychology for Modern Man'. In: *Collected Works of C.G. Jung Vol. 10 Civilisation in Transition*, p. 304.

— (1947) *On the Nature of the Psyche*. London: Ark Paperbacks.

— (1948) 'The Phenomenology of the Spirit in Fairy Tales'. In: *The Archetypes and the Collective Unconscious*, 9 (Part 1), pp. 207–54.

— (1953) *Collected Works Vol. 12. Psychology and Alchemy*. New York: Pantheon Books.

Maccoby, E.E. (1992) 'The Role of Parents in the Socialisation of Children: An Historical Overview'. In: *Developmental Psychology*, 28(6), pp. 1006–17.

Marks, I.M. (1978) 'Exposure Treatments: Clinical Applications'. In: *Behaviour Modification: Principles and Clinical Applications*. Boston: Little Brown & Co., pp. 204–42.

Maslow, A. (1954) *Motivation and Personality*. New York: Harper.

— (1962) *Toward a Psychology of Being*. New York: Van Nostrand.

Monahan, J., Steadman, H.J., Silver, E., Appelbaum, P.S., Robbins, P.C., Mulvey, E.P. and Banks, S. (2001) *Rethinking Risk Assessment: The MacArthur Study of Mental Disorder and Violence*. New York: Oxford University Press.

Pavlov, I.P. (1927) *Conditioned Reflexes: An Investigation of the Physiological Activity of the Cerebral Cortex*, trans. and ed. by G.V. Anrep. London: Oxford University Press.

— (1928) *Lectures on Conditioned Reflexes*, trans. by W.H. Gantt. London: Allen and Unwin.

Piaget, J. (1954) 'The Development of Object Concept', trans. by M. Cook. In: J. Piaget and M. Cook, *The Construction of Reality in the Child*. New York: Basic Books, pp. 3–96.

— (1954) 'The Child's Conception of Number'. In: *Journal of Consulting Psychology*, 18(1), 76.

— (1968) 'Quantification, Conservation, and Nativism'. In: *Science*, 162, pp. 976–9.

Piaget, J. and Szeminska, A. (1952) *The Child's Conception of Number*. Routledge & Kegan Paul: London.

Pierce, B. A. (2017) *Genetics: A Conceptual Approach*. New York: W.H. Freeman.

Snustad, D.P. and Simmons, M.J. (2015) *Principles of Genetics*. New Jersey: Wiley.

Rogers, C. (1951) *Client-Centred Therapy: Its Current Practice, Implications and Theory*. Boston: Houghton Mifflin.

— (1961) *On Becoming a Person: A Therapist's View of Psychotherapy*. Boston: Houghton Mifflin.

— (1963) 'The Concept of the Fully Functioning Person'. In: *Psychotherapy: Theory, Research & Practice*, 1(1), pp. 17–26.

— (1980) *A Way of Being*. Boston: Houghton Mifflin.

Rosenzweig, M.R., Breedlove, S.M. and Leiman, A.L. (2002) *Biological Psychology: An Introduction to Behavioural, Cognitive, and Clinical Neuroscience*. Massachusetts: Sinauer Associates.

Schaffer, R. (1996) *Social Development*. Oxford: Blackwell.

Schultz, D.P. and Schultz, S.E. (2011) A History of Modern Psychology. Canada: Cengage.

Simons, D. and Chabris, C. (1999) 'Gorillas in our Midst: Sustained Inattentional Blindness for Dynamic Events'. In: *Perception*, 28(9), pp. 1059–74.

Skinner, B.F. (1935) 'Two Types of Conditioned Reflex and a Pseudo Type'. In: *Journal of General Psychology*, 12, pp. 66–77.

— (1948) '"Superstition" in the Pigeon'. In: *Journal of Experimental Psychology*, 38, pp. 168–172.

— (1950) 'Are Theories of Learning Necessary?' In: *Psychological Review*, 57, pp. 193–216.

— (1971) *Beyond Freedom and Dignity*. Cambridge, MA: Hackett Publishing Co., Inc.

— (1989) 'The Origins of Cognitive Thought'. In: *American Psychologist*, 44, pp. 13–18.

The Psychological Society of Ireland, Code of Ethics. Available from: https://www.psychologicalsociety.ie/ [accessed 22 March 2022].

Thorndike, E.L. (1898) 'Animal Intelligence: An Experimental Study of the Associative Processes in Animals'. In: *Psychological Monographs: General and Applied*, 2(4), pp. i–109.

— (1905) *The Elements of Psychology*. New York: A.G. Seiler.

Tomarken, A.J., Mineka, S. and Cook, M. (1989) 'Fear-Relevant Selective Associations and Covariation Bias'. In: *Journal of Abnormal Psychology*, 98(4), p. 381.

Watson, J.B. (1913) 'Psychology as the Behaviourist Views It'. In: *Psychological Review*, 20, pp. 158–77.

Watson, J.B. and Rayner, R. (1920) 'Conditioned Emotional Reactions'. In: *Journal of Experimental Psychology*, 3(1), p. 1.

Vygotsky, L.S. (1962) *Thought and Language*. Cambridge MA: MIT Press.

— (1978) *Mind in Society: The Development of Higher Psychological Processes*. Cambridge, MA: Harvard University Press.

— (1987) 'Thinking and Speech'. In: R.W. Rieber and A.S. Carton (eds.), *The Collected Works of L.S. Vygotsky, Volume 1: Problems of General Psychology*. New York: Plenum Press, pp. 39–285.

Websites

https://www.cdc.gov/genomics/disease/epigenetics.htm#ref8

https://counsellingandtherapy.com/understanding-professional-regulation/

https://www.genome.gov/

https://www.hse.ie/

https://www.janegoodall.org/

https://www.mentalhealthireland.ie/research/

https://positivepsychology.com/

https://www.psychologicalsociety.ie/Article/Code-of-Ethics-1

USEFUL RESOURCES

ADHD Ireland https://adhdireland.ie/
Information and support for young people and adults with ADHD, for their parents/loved ones, and for professionals

Aware https://www.aware.ie/
An organisation that 'undertakes to create a society where people affected by stress, depression, bipolar disorder and mood-related conditions are understood, supported, free from stigma, and are encouraged to access appropriate therapies'

Bodywhys https://www.bodywhys.ie/
Support services for people suffering from eating disorders, information on treatment and professional and educational services

Coru https://www.coru.ie/
Regulating health and social care professionals, '[protecting] the public by promoting high standards of professional conduct, education, training and competence'

Headspace https://www.headspace.com/
Meditation and mindfulness app

Healthy Ireland https://www.hse.ie/healthandwellbeing/
A government-led initiative which aims to 'create an Irish society where everyone can enjoy physical and mental health, and where wellbeing is valued and supported at every level of society'

USEFUL RESOURCES

Health Service Executive	https://www2.hse.ie/healthy-you/minding-your-wellbeing-programme.html From HSE Health and Wellbeing, an 'evidence-based programme [providing] a unique opportunity for people to learn more about mindfulness, gratitude, self-care and resilience'
Inclusion Ireland	https://inclusionireland.ie/ National association for people with an intellectual disability, whose mission is to 'champion the rights of people with an intellectual disability in Ireland through securing the full implementation of the United Nations Convention on the Rights of Persons with Disabilities (UN CRPD)'
Jigsaw	https://jigsaw.ie/ Mental health service offering advice and support to young people aged 12–25 years
LGBT	https://lgbt.ie/ Support service for the LGBT community
Mental Health Ireland	https://www.mentalhealthireland.ie/ Mental health charity whose aim is to promote positive mental health, wellbeing and recovery
Pieta House	https://www.pieta.ie/ Professional one-to-one therapeutic service to people who are in suicidal distress, those who engage in self-harm, and those bereaved by suicide
Shine	https://shine.ie/ Support service for people affected by mental ill health

Spun Out	https://spunout.ie/ Youth-led information website about the importance of holistic wellbeing and how good health can be maintained, both physically and mentally
Yoga with Adriene	www.youtube.com/yogawithadriene Popular YouTube channel providing yoga classes for all levels

INDEX

A
ABC technique 62–3, 68, 90
abnormal behaviour 106–9
  dangerous 106, 108, 160
  deviant 106, 107–8, 160
  diagnosing 109–10
  distress 106, 107, 160
  dysfunction 106–7, 160
abnormal disorders 110–11
abnormal psychology 105–12
  abnormal behaviour, determining 106–9
  abnormal behaviour, diagnosing 109–10
  abnormal disorders 110–11
  criticisms of 112
  definition 105
  therapeutic interventions 111–12
accommodation 60, 165
acetylcholine 73
ADHD (attention deficit hyperactivity disorder) 72, 87
adolescents/adolescence 102, 134
  case studies 133, 141, 143
  characteristics 102
  identity versus role confusion 32
  peer relationships 102, 133, 162
adrenal glands 80, 81
adulthood 33, 103
Ainsworth, Mary 91, 92–4
  developmental psychology 91, 92–4
  Strange Situation experiment 92–4, 160–1
ambivert 26
American crowbar case 75
American Psychological Association 2
amygdala 77, 165
anal compulsive 17, 165
anal expulsive 17, 165
anal fixation 17
anima 25, 165
animus 25, 165
Anna Freud Centre 23
anorexia nervosa 110
anxiety disorders 2, 13, 46, 65, 85, 87, 110
archetypes
  (1) the persona 25
  (2) the shadow 25
  (3) the anima/animus 25
  (4) the self 25
  concept 165
  Jungian archetypes 25
  see also personality archetypes
Aristotle 5
art therapy 37–8, 89
Asperger's 110
assimilation 59, 165
attachment styles 92–4, 161
  disorganised attachment 94, 161
  insecure-avoidant attachment 93, 161
  insecure-resistant attachment 93–4, 161
  secure attachment 93, 161
  strange situation procedure 92–4, 160–1
attachment theory 34–5, 85
attention deficit hyperactivity disorder see ADHD

autism spectrum disorder 110
autonomic nervous system 79–80
aversion therapy 46, 89, 165

B
basal ganglia 77
Baumrind, Diana 91, 94–6, 155, 159
Beck, Aaron 2, 63–6, 90
behaviourism 2, 39–47, 89, 165
   aversive conditioning 46
   classical conditioning 40–2
   concept 165
   criticisms of 47, 89
   exposure therapy 46
   Little Albert experiment 42–3, 118, 163–4
   operant conditioning 44–6, 137, 154
   Pavlov's dog 39–40
   systemic desensitisation 47
   therapeutic interventions 46–7
Bernays, Martha 23
biological evolution 82–3
biological psychology 70–88, 90
   central nervous system 73–7
   criticisms of 87–8, 90
   definition 70
   endocrine system 80–2
   genetic psychology 83–7
   human nervous system 70–80
   peripheral nervous system 78–80
   therapeutic interventions 87
biopsychology 4
bipolar disorder 72, 87, 110
Bobo Doll experiment 125
bonding 34–5
Bouchard, T. J and McGue, M. 86
Bowlby, John 22, 34–6, 85, 92
   attachment theory 34–5, 154
   bonding 34–5
   maternal deprivation theory 35–6

brain 73, 74–7
   American crowbar case 75
   basal ganglia 77
   brainstem 74
   cerebellum 74
   cerebrum 74
   frontal lobes 75
   hypothalamus 76, 80
   limbic system 76, 77
   lobes of 75–6
   meninges 73
   occipital lobes 76
   parietal lobes 76
   pineal gland 77, 80
   pituitary gland 76, 80
   temporal lobes 76
   thalamus 77
   Wernicke's area 76
Briggs, Katherine 26
Broca, Paul 75
Broca's area 75, 166
Bronfenbrenner, Urie 91, 97–8, 135, 156
Bruner, Jerome 2
bulimia nervosa 110

C
case studies
   ecological systems 98–9, 135–6, 137–8
   emotional turmoil 141
   Maslow's Hierarchy of Needs 135, 136
   psychosocial development 34
   school stress/mental health 143
   self-esteem issues 139–40
catharsis 9, 166
causation 117, 166
CBT (cognitive behavioural therapy) 62–6, 68, 90, 111, 138, 158, 159, 166

cognitive distortions 64–6, 158
cognitive therapy 62, 63–6
REBT 62–3, 68, 90, 111, 169
central nervous system (CNS) 73–7, 159
Charcot, Jean 10
child psychoanalysis 2, 22–3
classical conditioning 40–2, 89, 166
    conditioned response 42
    conditioned stimulus 41
    extinction 42, 167
    generalisation 42
    neutral stimulus 41, 42, 43
    unconditioned response 41, 42, 43, 170
    unconditioned stimulus 41, 42, 43, 170
client-centred therapy 51–4
clinical psychology 4
CNS *see* central nervous system
cognition 158
cognitive behavioural therapy *see* CBT
cognitive development
    (1) sensorimotor stage 58, 60, 61
    (2) preoperational stage 58, 60, 61
    (3) concrete operational stage 59, 60, 61
    (4) formal operational stage 59, 60, 61, 133
    accommodation 60
    assimilation 59
    equilibrium and disequilibrium 60
    schema 59
    stages of 58–9, 60–1, 154, 159
cognitive dissonance 90
cognitive distortions 64–6, 158
    black-and-white thinking 65, 158
    catastrophising 65, 158
    definition 158
    jumping to conclusions 65, 158
    over-generalisation 65, 158
    personalisation 66
    'should' statements 66
cognitive psychology 2, 57–69, 90
    cognitive development, Piaget's theory 58–61
    criticisms of 69, 90
    definition 57, 154
    therapeutic interventions 68
cognitive therapy 62, 63–6
cognitive triad 63–4, 90
collective unconscious 24, 25, 27, 165, 166
comparative psychology 4
congruence 54, 166
consciousness 166
consciousness, theory of 11–12
correlation 117, 166
correlational research design 115, 117–18
counselling psychology 4
cultural psychology 2

D

dangerous behaviour 106, 108
Darwin, Charles 7, 82–3, 90
Dawkins, Richard 2
defence mechanisms 13–15, 23, 159
    definition 13, 156, 166
    denial 13–14, 157
    displacement 14, 157
    projection 14, 157
    rationalisation 15, 157
    reaction formation 14
    regression 14, 157
    repression 14, 157
    sublimation 14, 157
denial 13–14, 157
deoxyribonucleic acid *see* DNA
depression/depressive disorders 63–4, 110, 112
    drug therapy 2, 87, 160

Descartes, René 5
descriptive research design 115–17
developmental psychology 4, 91–104, 159
　attachment styles 92–4, 161
　criticisms of 104
　definition 91
　ecological systems 97–9
　lifespan development 99–103
　parenting styles 94–6
　therapeutic interventions 103
deviant behaviour 106, 107–8
Dewey, John 7
Diagnostic and Statistical Manual, The see DSM
displacement 14, 157
distress 106, 107
DNA (deoxyribonucleic acid) 83, 86, 166
dopamine 72
dream analysis 2, 19–20, 27–8, 37, 89, 166
drugs/drug therapy 90, 112
　anti-anxiety drugs 87
　antidepressants 87
　antipsychotic drugs 87
　in biological psychology 87
　depressive disorders 2, 87, 160
　mood stabilisers 87
　psychostimulants 87
DSM (*Diagnostic and Statistical Manual, The*) 2, 109, 166
DSM-I 109
DSM-II 2
DSM-III 2
DSM-IV 2
DSM-V 109, 110, 159
Dutch famine (1944–5) 86
dysfunction 106–7

E

ecological systems 97–9, 156
　case studies 98–9, 135–6, 137–8
　exosystem 97, 137, 156
　macrosystem 88, 97, 137, 156
　mesosystem 97, 137, 156
　microsystem 97, 137
　sample exam answer 156
　sample exam question 147
ECT (electroconvulsive therapy) 87, 88, 90, 112
educational psychology 4
ego
　Freud and 15, 17, 167
　Jung and 24, 167
Electra complex 18, 167
electroconvulsive therapy *see* ECT
Elkind, David 102
Ellis, Albert, REBT 62–3, 90, 169
endocrine system 80–2, 90
enteric nervous system 80
epigenetics 87–8, 90
equilibrium and disequilibrium 60
Erikson, Erik Homburger 22, 29–33, 89, 91, 99, 133, 162
　psychosocial development theory 29–33, 162
erogenous zone 16, 17, 18, 19, 167
Ethical Principles of Psychologists and Code of Conduct (APA) 2
ethics 167
ethics in psychology 121–3, 162–3
　(1) respect for the rights and dignity of the person 122, 162
　(2) competence 122, 163
　(3) responsibility 122–3, 163
　(4) integrity 123, 163
　healthy boundaries 129–30
　PSI Code of Professional Ethics 122–3, 162–3

ethics in research 123–4
    see also unethical research
evolutionary psychology 2
exam questions with answers
    paper 1 answers 154–8
    paper 1 questions 145–9
    paper 2 answers 159–64
    paper 2 questions 150–3
experimental psychology 4, 6
experimental research design 118–19
exposure therapy 46, 89
extinction 42, 167
extrovert 25, 26, 167

F
Facial Expressions experiment 125
feeding disorders 110
fixations 16, 17, 18, 167
Food and Drug Administration (FDA) 2
forensic psychology 4
free association
    Freud and 9–10, 20, 89, 167
    technique 36–7, 167
Freud, Anna 2, 22–3, 29, 89
Freud, Sigmund 9–20, 22, 23, 24, 25, 89, 99
    criticism of 38
    defence mechanisms 13–15, 156, 159
    dream analysis 19–20, 166
    ego 15, 17, 167
    Electra complex 18, 167
    erogenous zone 16, 17, 18, 19, 167
    fixation 16, 167
    free association 9–10, 12, 20, 89, 167
    human mind: mental iceberg 11
    id 15, 17, 168
    Interpretation of Dreams, The 2
    libido 16, 19, 168

Oedipus complex 17–18, 169
personality theory 12–13
psychosexual development, stages of 15–19, 133
superego 15, 16, 17, 18, 89, 155, 170
theory of consciousness 11–12
Freudian slip 12, 167
functionalism 2, 7

G
Gage, Phineas 75
genetic psychology 83–7, 90
genetics 83–6, 168
genotype prediction 84
Gestalt psychology 2, 48
Gibbs' Reflective Cycle 132
glutamate 72
Goodall, Jane 2, 85, 90

H
Harlow, Harry 35, 84–5, 90
health psychology 4
hormones
    endocrine system and 81, 82, 90
    hypothalamus and 76
    insulin 81
    norepinephrine 72
    oestrogen 82
    pituitary gland and 77
    production and secretion 76, 77
    progesterone 82
    testosterone 82
human genome mapping 2
human mind, Freud's view of 11
human nervous system 70–80, 90
    central nervous system 73–7
    peripheral nervous system 78–80
humanistic psychology 2, 48–56, 90, 138, 168
    client-centred therapy, Rogers and 51–4

congruence and incongruence 54
criticisms of 56, 90
Maslow's hierarchy of needs 49–51
mindfulness 55
person-centred therapy 54
play therapy 55
self-concept, Rogers' theory of 54
therapeutic interventions 54–5
transpersonal therapy 55, 159
hypnosis 9
hypothalamus 76, 80, 81, 168
hypothesis 168
hysteria 9, 10

I

id 15, 17, 168
ideal self 53, 54
identity crisis 29
imprinting, theory of 35
incongruence 54, 168
infancy 100
International Classification of Diseases 11th Revision (ICD 11) 110
interpersonal skills 127–9
    case study 133–4, 138
    communication 127
    creativity 129
    empathy 128
    flexibility 129
    honesty 128
    kindness 128
    patience 128
    self-awareness 128
    validation 128
introvert 25–6, 168

J

James, William 2, 7, 57
    Principles of Psychology, The 7
Johnson, Wendell 124

Jung, Carl Gustav 22, 23–8
    archetypes 25
    collective unconscious 24, 25, 27, 165, 166
    dream analysis 27–8
    ego 24, 167
    extrovert 25, 26, 167
    personal unconscious 24, 169
    personality archetypes 27–8
    personality theory 25–6

K

Klein, Melanie 36
Koffka, Kurt 2

L

law of effect 44
libido 16, 19, 168
lifespan development 99–103
    adolescence 102, 134
    adulthood 103
    infancy 100
    prenatal development 99–100
    preschool 101
    school-age child 101
    toddler 100–1
limbic system 76, 77
Little Albert experiment 42–3, 118, 163–4
Locke, John 5
Lorenz, Konrad 35

M

Maccoby, E.E. 95
Maslow, Abraham 2, 48–51, 90
Maslow's Hierarchy of Needs 49–51, 90, 155
    belongingness and love needs 50
    case studies 135, 136, 139, 141, 143
    esteem needs 50, 155
    physiological needs 50, 155

safety needs 50, 155
self-actualisation 49, 50, 51, 136, 155
 social 155
maternal deprivation theory 35–6
melatonin 77, 169
Mendel, Gregor 83–4, 90
Mental Health Ireland 106
Milgram conformity experiment 124–5
Milgram, Stanley 124–5
Miller, George A. 2
mindfulness 55, 138
MKO (more knowledgeable other) 67, 168
monotropy 35, 168
 Monster Study 124
mood disorders 2, 87, 110, 112
more knowledgeable other see MKO
Myers, Isabel 26
Myers-Briggs personality test 26

N
naturalistic observations 115, 116
nature-nurture debate 5, 67
negative self-schemas 64
Neisser, Ulric 2
neo-Freudianism 22–38
 Bowlby, John 22, 34–36, 35–6, 85, 92, 154
 Erikson, Erik 29–33
 Freud, Anna 2, 23, 29, 89
 Jung, Carl 23–8, 27, 165, 166
 therapeutic interventions 36–8
neuroendocrine system 77
neurons 71, 79, 168
 motor neurons 71, 79
 sensory neurons 71, 79
neurotransmitters 71–3, 90, 169
norepinephrine 72

O
obsessive compulsive disorder (OCD) 110
Oedipus complex 17–18, 169
operant conditioning 44–6, 89, 137, 154, 169
 negative punishment 46
 negative reinforcement 46
 positive punishment 46
 positive reinforcement 45, 154
 Skinner box 45
oral fixation 16, 17, 21
Organisation for Economic Co-operation and Development (OECD) 105
organisational psychology 4
ovaries 80, 81, 82

P
pancreas 80, 81
parasympathetic nervous system 79
parenting styles 94–5, 155
 authoritarian 95, 96, 155
 authoritative 94, 95, 96, 155
 case studies 96
 permissive 95, 96, 155
 uninvolved/neglectful 95
Pavlov, Ivan 39–41
Pearson correlation coefficient 117
peer relationships
 adolescents and 102, 133, 162
 school-age children and 101
penis envy 18
peripheral nervous system 78–80
 autonomic nervous system 79–80
 enteric nervous system 80
 somatic nervous system 79
person-centred therapy 54, 90
personal unconscious 24, 169

personality archetypes 24, 27–9, 38, 159
  (1) ruler 27
  (2) creator 27, 28
  (3) sage 27, 28
  (4) innocent 27
  (5) explorer 27, 28
  (6) rebel 27
  (7) hero 27, 28
  (8) wizard 28
  (9) jester 28
  (10) everyman 28
  (11) lover 28
  (12) caregiver 28
personality disorders 111
personality test 26
personality theory 12–13, 25–6
  (1) the persona 25
  (2) the shadow 25
  (3) the anima/animus 26
  (4) the self 25
  archetypes 25
philosophy 4–5
Piaget, Jean 2, 58–61
  accommodation, concept of 60
  assimilation, concept of 59
  cognitive development, stages of 60–1, 90, 133, 154, 159
  equilibrium and disequilibrium 60
  schema, concept of 59, 169
pineal gland 77, 80, 81, 169
Pit of Despair experiment 84–5
pituitary gland 77, 80, 81, 169
Plato 5
play therapy 23, 37, 55, 89, 138
positive psychology 2
prenatal development 99–100
preschool children 101
primates, studies of 2, 84–5
projection 14, 157

PSI Code of Professional Ethics 122–3, 162–3
psyche 4, 23
  collective unconscious 24
  ego 24
  personal unconscious 24
psychoanalysis 2, 9–10, 36–8, 89
  art therapy 37–8
  criticisms of 38, 89
  dream analysis 19–20, 37
  free association 9–10, 36–7
  play therapy 37, 137
  theorists 155
  transference 37
Psychological Society of Ireland (PSI) 121, 162
  PSI Code of Professional Ethics 122–3, 162–3
psychology
  branches 4
  earliest schools of 6–7
  origins of 4–5
  perspectives 1, 3
  research methods 113–20
  timeline of 2
psychosexual development 15–19
  (1) oral stage 16–17, 19
  (2) anal stage 17, 19
  (3) phallic stage 17, 19
  (4) latency stage 18
  (5) genital stage 18, 19, 133
psychosocial stages of development 30–3
  (1) trust versus mistrust 30–1
  (2) autonomy versus shame and doubt 31
  (3) initiative versus guilt 31
  (4) industry versus inferiority 32–3
  (5) identity versus role confusion 32
  (6) intimacy versus isolation 32
  (7) generativity versus stagnation 33

(8) integrity versus despair 33
psychotic disorders 111
Punnett, Reginald C. 84

Q
qualitative data 114–15, 116, 117, 169
quantitative data 114, 115, 116, 117, 169

R
rational emotive behavioural therapy
    see REBT
rationalisation 15, 157
Rayner, Rosalie 43
reaction formation 14
REBT (rational emotive behavioural
    therapy) 62–3, 68, 90, 111, 169
reflection 131–2
regression 14, 157
repression 14, 157
research methods in psychology
    113–20
    correlational research design
        117–18
    descriptive research design 115–17
    experimental research design
        118–19
    qualitative and quantitative data
        114–15
    scientific method 113–15, 116–17
    sources, primary and secondary 115
    sources, validity and reliability of
        119–20
    types of research design 115–19
Rogers, Carl 2, 51–4, 89, 90
    congruence 54, 166
    incongruence 54, 168
    self-actualisation 169
    self-concept 51, 53, 169
    unconditional positive regard 52,
        54, 170

S
schema 59, 169
schizophrenia 87, 111
school-age children 101
self-actualisation 90, 169
    Maslow's hierarchy of needs and
        49, 50, 51, 136, 155
    Rogers' concept and 51, 54, 56, 169
self-care 130–1
self-concept 51, 53, 169
self-esteem 53, 54
    case study 139–40
self-image 53, 54
Seligman, Martin 2
serotonin 72
Skinner, B.F. 2, 44–6, 89, 169
    operant conditioning 44–6, 89, 169
sociocultural theory 67
Socrates 5
somatic nervous system 79
Spencer, Herbert 83
sports psychology 4
Stanford Prison experiment 125
Strange Situation experiment 92–4,
    160
stress 65, 72, 80
structuralism 2, 6–7, 48
sublimation 14, 157
superego 15, 16, 17, 18, 155, 170
sympathetic nervous system 79, 80
systemic desensitisation 47, 89

T
teratogen 99, 170
testes 80, 82
thalamus 77
therapists
    case study 133–4
    interpersonal skills 127–9
    reflection 131–2
    self-care 130–1

therapist-client relationship 129–30
Thorndike, Edward 44
thymus 80, 81
thyroid gland 80, 81
Titchener, Edward 2, 6
toddlers 100–1
transference 12, 37, 89, 170
transpersonal therapy 55, 159
Tudor, Mary 124
twin studies 85–6, 90

U

UCLA Schizophrenic experiments 125
unconditional positive regard 52, 54, 170
unconditioned response 41, 43, 170
unconditioned stimulus 41, 42, 43, 170
unethical research 124–5, 163–4

V

variable 114, 117, 118, 119, 170
Vygotsky, Lev 67–8, 90
   MKO (more knowledgeable other) 67, 168
   zone of proximal development 67, 154

W

Watson, John Broadus 2, 39, 42–3, 89, 118
Wernicke, Carl 76
Wernicke's area 75, 76, 170
Wertheimer, Max 48–9
World Health Organization (WHO) 110
Wundt, Wilhelm 2, 6–7, 48, 57

Z

zone of proximal development (ZPD) 67, 154